# NIGHT FIGHTER ACES OF THE LUFTWAFFE 1943–45

CASEMATE | ILLUSTRATED

CASEMATE | ILLUSTRATED

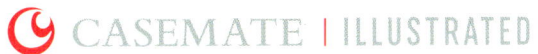

# NIGHT FIGHTER ACES OF THE LUFTWAFFE 1943–45

NEIL PAGE AND JEAN-LOUIS ROBA

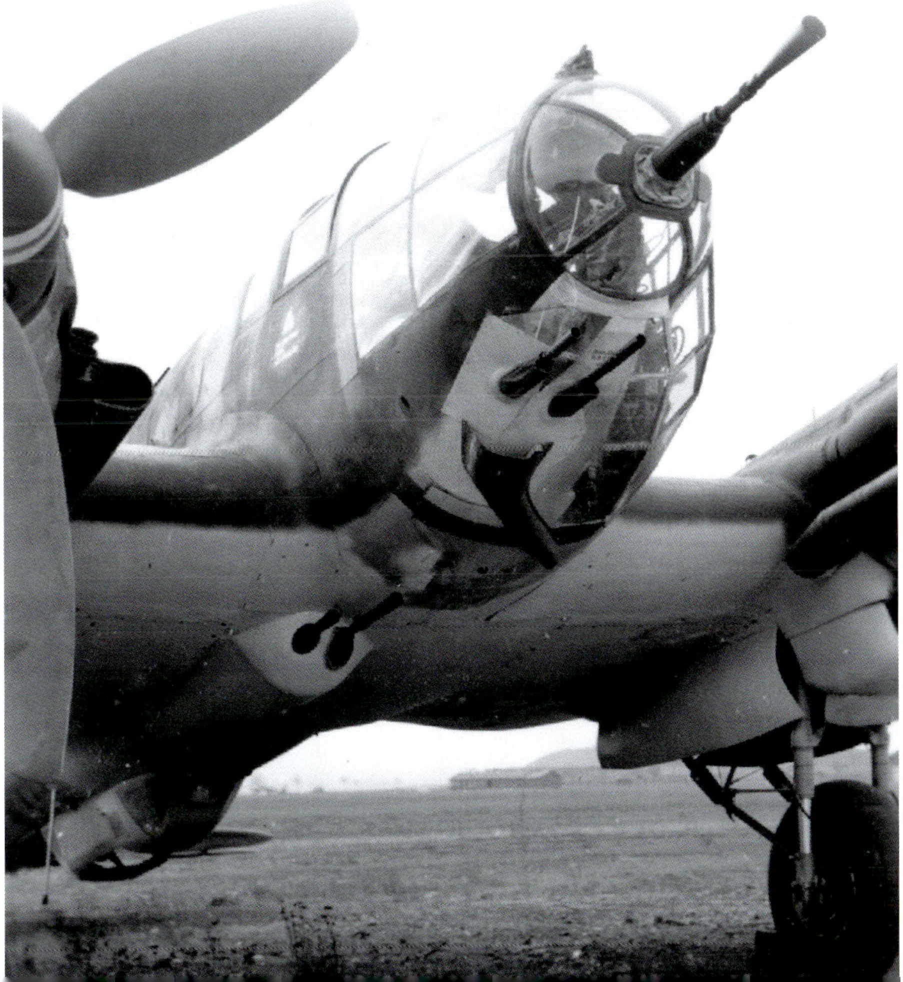

# CASEMATE | ILLUSTRATED

CIS0058

Published in 2025 by
CASEMATE PUBLISHERS
1950 Lawrence Road, Havertown, PA 19083, USA
and
47 Church Street, Barnsley, S70 2AS, UK

Print Edition: ISBN 978-1-63624-554-6
Digital Edition: ISBN 978-1-63624-555-3

© 2025 Neil Page and Jean-Louis Roba

All rights reserved. No part of this book may be reproduced or transmitted in any form or by any means, electronic or mechanical including photocopying, recording or by any information storage and retrieval system, without permission from the publisher in writing.

Design by Battlefield Design
Aircraft profiles by Claes Sundin
Printed and bound in the Czech Republic by FINIDR s.r.o.

CASEMATE PUBLISHERS (US)
Telephone (610) 853-9131
Fax (610) 853-9146
Email: casemate@casematepublishers.com
www.casematepublishers.com

CASEMATE PUBLISHERS (UK)
Telephone (0)1226 734350
Email: casemate@casemateuk.com
www.casemateuk.com

Author's note: As the subject of this book is Luftwaffe night fighter aces, the authors have concentrated on the "regular" NJG units. Other units engaged in night combat—like those of the *Wilde Sau* (JG 300 to 302) or highly specialized Staffeln, such as the Me 410s of V./KG 2 or KG 51)—are mentioned where appropriate, but lack of space precludes more detailed coverage. Monthly Nachtjagd losses are only indicative, as the official listings do not always specify the cause.

Photo credits: Neil Page wishes to acknowledge the generous assistance of Theo Boiten, Paul Stipdonk, Delmar Davis, and Ron Ferguson in compiling this volume.

Title page: A closeup of the forward-firing armament installed in the nose of Oblt Günther Bertram's He 111—five 2-cm cannon. This machine was deployed by the Nachtjagd *Schwarm* of Luftflotte 6. (Theo Boiten)
Contents page photo: *Punchboard* was Barte's 16th victory.
Map: Luftwaffe aerial photo of Timisoara, Romania (Temeschburg in German), October 1944. Strategic targets are highlighted on the map, including the marshaling yard, fuel depots, and various bridges.

The Publisher's authorised representative in the EU for product safety is Authorised Rep Compliance Ltd., Ground Floor, 71 Lower Baggot Street, Dublin D02 P593, Ireland. www.arccompliance.com

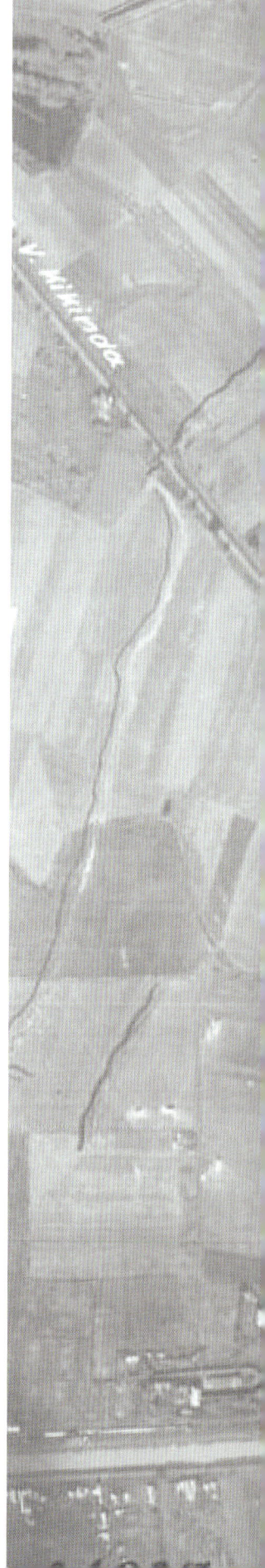

# Contents

Timeline of Events ................................... 6
Introduction ........................................... 10
Reinforcing the Nachtjagd Ost: July–September 1943 ............................... 11
In the West: August–December 1943 ............. 18
The Battle for Berlin: November 1943–March 1944 .................................... 34
The Normandy Campaign: June–August 1944 ................................................. 60
In the East: January–September 1944 ............. 81
In the West: September 1944–January 1, 1945 ................................................. 90
Terminal Decline: January–May 1945 .......... 106
Afterword ............................................ 124
References and Further Reading ................ 125
Index ................................................... 126

# Timeline of Events

The last two years of the war proved increasingly fraught for the Nachtjagdgeschwader. Although the bravery and tenacity of the night fighters was rarely called into question and the tactical innovations of the Nachtjagd unmatched, Luftwaffe strategy and German production could not keep pace with Allied supremacy that was manifest in almost every department. From mid-1943, despite impressive numbers of Nachtjagd victories, the night fighters flew increasingly by day against USAF bombers and from mid-1944 onwards were virtually a nighttime extension of the Schlacht arm, committed to ground-attack sorties both in the West as the Allies rolled across France and in the East as the Russians swarmed across Poland and drove into East Prussia. The Nachtjagd took part in the ill-fated *Wacht am Rhein* during December 1944, the last German offensive in the West. Nachtjagd Ju 88s also flew the *Bodenplatte* mission—the attack on Allied airfields on New Year's Day 1945—which saw the largest force of German fighters ever assembled take to the air. Two hundred Luftwaffe aircraft were lost in a morning.

The Nachtjagd swansong, Operation *Gisela*, on March 3/4, 1945, was a futile attempt to repeat the "intruder" successes of the early war years by crippling the RAF over England as the bombers returned from a raid. The Nachtjagdgeschwader claimed only 24 RAF aircraft destroyed and nine damaged. Their own losses were 22 and 12 respectively.

By this stage of the war a Staffel of Me 262 jet fighters was also flying nocturnal missions—chasing RAF Mosquitos in the night skies over Berlin. A handful of skilled pilots flew the single-seater Me262 A and on the night of March 27/28, 1945, the radar-equipped Me 262 B-1a/U1 twin-seater flew its first nighttime sortie. The aircraft was lost after the engines flamed out. Over the next six weeks or so, some 50 Nachtjagd Staffeln were disbanded and their personnel sent to fight with ground forces, signaling the end of the night fighter arm of the Luftwaffe.

**August 1, 1943:** The first *Alarmstart* (scramble) received by the new IV./NJG 6—a daylight sortie to counter *Tidal Wave*—a USAAF mission targeting the Ploesti oilfields in Romania.

**August 2/3, 1943:** The final raid of the combined RAF/USAAF assault on Hamburg—Operation *Gomorrah*.

**August 17, 1943:** USAAF bombers mount an ambitious raid on Schweinfurt and Regensburg. More than 100 night fighters sent up.

Last Kommandeur of IV./NJG 6, Hptm Martin Becker flew this Bf 110 G-4 abandoned in Neubiberg where it was photographed by American troops. The tailfin featured 43 *Abschussbalken* victory markings indicating the date of the last two as September 12, 1944. Becker flew a Ju 88 G-6 for subsequent sorties/kills which was also coded "MF." On the night of March 14/15, 1945, Becker and his crew set a Nachtjagd record of nine claims for one night, kills 49–57. This included three credited to BF Johanssen using the defensive rear-facing MG 131 Z after the forward-firing armament failed. (Crow collection)

**August 31, 1943**: New Eastern Front Nachtjagdgeschwader NJG 100 and NJG 200 feature in Luftwaffe organization charts

**October 1, 1943**: Establishment of JG 301, the *Wilde Sau* units, organized under the direction of "Hajo" Herrmann's new 30 Jagddivision.

**November 17/18, 1943**: A small force is dispatched by Bomber Command to Ludwigshafen to test the new improved H2S ground-scanning radar system, known as H2S Mk III. Maj. Walter Ehle, Kommandeur of II./NJG 1, is killed in a crash-landing at St.-Trond.

**November 18, 1943**: "Bomber" Harris opens the Battle of Berlin—between this date and March 25, 1944, Berlin is subjected to a series of 16 major raids.

**December 29/30, 1943**: The last raid on Berlin in 1943 comprises 457 Lancasters, 252 Halifaxes and three Mosquitos—18 bombers are shot down bringing total RAF losses for 1943 to 2,225 bombers downed with over 5,000 more damaged.

**January 21/22, 1944:** The Nachtjagd suffers a grievous loss with the death in action of Hptm. Heinrich Prinz zu Sayn-Wittgenstein, Kommodore of NJG 2.

**March 1/2, 1944:** 577 bombers attack Stuttgart, losing only four aircraft.

**March 6, 1944:** During the first large-scale day raid on Berlin by the USAAF, five B-17s are brought down by night fighters.

**March 6/7, 1944:** Lt. Klaus Scheer of 4./NJG 100 downs five Soviet PS-84s in the Narva area (Estonia), his most successful night of the war.

**March 15, 1944:** Kommodore NJG 6, Maj. Heinrich Wohlers, an ace with 29 victories, is killed in a crash at Echterdingen.

**March 30/31, 1944:** The RAF launch a "maximum effort" raid on Nuremberg, the "City of the NSDAP." 795 aircraft are dispatched—572 Lancasters, 214 Halifaxes, and nine Mosquitos. Nearly 100 bombers are lost and over 500 Commonwealth airmen perish, the RAF's biggest loss of the war.

**May 5, 1944:** The USAAF launch 446 B-17s over Ploesti by day and RAF 205 Group dispatch Wellingtons and Halifaxes over the refineries by night. Kommandeur IV./NJG 6 Lütje claims his 33rd victory.

**May 6/7, 1944:** Oblt. Werner Baake, Staka of 2./NJG 1 downs an LNSF Mosquito returning from Leverkusen, the first Mosquito to be credited to a Heinkel He 219.

**May–June 1944:** In the runup to and the weeks following D-Day, RAF Bomber Command carries out large-scale raids in France and Belgium on communications hubs, bridges, roads, and V1 rocket launch sites.

**July 8, 1944:** Baranovichi, a long-term NJG 100 operating base, is retaken by the Soviets.

**July 22, 1944:** The huge Soviet offensive *Bagration* collapses the Eastern Front forcing three German armies into headlong retreat.

**August 1, 1944:** The Polish Resistance Movement start their uprising in Warsaw—the fighting lasts 63 days.

**August 16/17, 1944:** Highest-scoring Eastern Front ace Lt. Gustav Francsi (1./NJG 100) claims four RAF *Viermots* attempting to resupply Warsaw.

## Timeline of Events

**August 20–23, 1944:** The Romanian–German front cracks under the pressure of two Soviet armies and on August 23, Romania changes sides. The Wehrmacht evacuates the country.

**October 5, 1944:** Obstlt. Helmut Lent, Kommodore of NJG 3 and victor in 110 air combats, crashes at Paderborn and dies of his injuries two days later. Göring gives the funeral oration.

**December 16, 1944:** The Wehrmacht launches *Wacht am Rhein*, an offensive aimed at the port of Antwerp. 17 Gruppen from the NJGs 1, 2, 3, 4, 5, and 6 fly *Nachtschlachteinsätze* (night ground-attack sorties).

**January 1, 1945:** *Bodenplatte*—the attack on Allied airfields in Belgium. NJG Ju 88s serve as guides ("*Lotse*") for Tagjagd formations often made up of fledgling pilots unable to find their way around. The Luftwaffe sustains very heavy losses.

**January 25, 1945:** "Kommando Welter" is "officially" designated 10./NJG 11 with a typical Staffel-strength establishment of 12 Me 262s.

**March 3/4, 1945:** Operation *Gisela*, the Nachtjagd swansong. Some 80 Ju 88 night fighters from NJG 2, III. and IV./NJG 3, NJG 4, and III./NJG 5 "hunt" RAF bombers over England as they return from a raid on Germany.

**February 13/14, 1945:** The RAF bombing of Dresden, with 20,000 civilians killed. There are only two victories for the Nachtjagd.

**March–April 1945:** Some 50 Nachtjagd Staffeln are disbanded, and their personnel sent to fight with ground forces.

**March 16/17, 1945:** Bomber Command's twin-pronged assault on the southern German cities of Nuremberg and Würzburg, with 300 heavy bombers assigned to strike at each. In a 30-minute period "swimming in the stream" Lt. Erich Jung's 5./NJG 2 crew claims eight Lancasters shot down.

**May 2/3, 1945:** Oblt. Fritz Brandt of the Stab/NJG 3 shoots down a 199 Sqn Halifax north of Hamburg, his eighth *Abschuss* and the last Nachtjagd victory of the war.

# Introduction

The week-long Allied bombing campaign against Hamburg in late July 1943 was not only hugely destructive but also had a significant impact on the German night fighter arm. From now on, the "boxes" of Kammhuber's *Raumnachtjagd*—lit. night fighter sectors—would be the starting point from which fighters would be led into the bomber stream as early as possible, a tactic dubbed *Zahme Sau*. The night fighters had to quickly adopt new "freelance" procedures and found themselves increasingly engaged in daylight operations. These actions resulted in heavy losses—especially of experienced aces—which the Nachtjagd could ill afford and struggled to replace.

The winter of 1943/44 saw a series of massive raids on Berlin. Although hard pressed, the Nachtjagd aces were still able to score some heavy tactical victories. Over a thousand RAF *Viermots* were shot down—more than double the expected losses—before the campaign was cut short. New night fighter aces emerged, often former transport and reconnaissance pilots, and the upward-firing armament of the Bf 110s and Ju 88s could cut swathes through the stream.

However, by mid-1944, as the Allies advanced, the night fighter aces were forced into new roles, including ground-strafing armor and troop concentrations, a role for which they were clearly unsuited. A small number of Me 262 jets were deployed in a new NJG 11, but exclusively committed against the rapid twin-engine Mosquitos of the RAF's Light Night Striking Force (LNSF). Heinkel He 219s were never available in significant numbers and prowling Mosquito intruders were an ever-present danger to Nachtjagd crews.

While the surviving night fighter aces continued their defensive actions virtually every night, by early 1945 the Nachtjagd was in terminal decline. Of the 1,100 night fighter pilots and crew who claimed at least one victory, some 669 were lost, a casualty rate of around 60 percent.

# Reinforcing the Nachtjagd Ost: July–September 1943

Up to this point, Luftwaffe night fighting in the East had been ridiculously piecemeal. This was due to the impossibility of creating any permanent infrastructure (Würzburg installations, guidance centers, etc.) Improvisation was the order of the day. This was a different type of night fighting, which even extended to employing He 111s as "night fighters" operating in independent *Schwärme* or "flights," as Obolt. Günther Bertram recalled:

> the so-called Nachtjagdschwärme Ost were formed from a single crew selected from each *Kampfgeschwader*. A crew was also made available from the *Fernaufklärer* [long-range reconnaissance] under Oblt. Wolfgang Schneeweiss. As the first *Schwarm* only comprised three machines (two He 111s and a single Ju 88), fuel and munitions replenishment, along with maintenance and servicing requirements for the aircraft were always undertaken at the airfield of whichever larger unit we happened to be operating from. As luck would have it, in Sestchinskaya this happened to be my old unit KG 4, while later in Smolensk we were based on the field used by a Nachtaufklärungsstaffel and later still in Orsha we came under the umbrella of the Fernaufklärungsstaffel, with which our Schwarmführer Oblt. Schneeweiss had previously seen service (note; FAG 2). It was while operating from Orsha that the Schwarmführer failed to return from a sortie.

Schneeweiss was posted MIA on the night of July 28/29, 1943. Recommended for the RK, his achievements in the Nachtjagd Ost amounted to as many as 15 night victories in the He 111, including two Li-2s on the night of July 26/27. Bertram took over the *Schwarm*:

> I achieved three victories while flying out of Orsha over the Kursk salient. We were hard on the heels of three "Maxim Gorky" four-engine bombers that had been caught in searchlights operated by the flak, which they had managed to evade. Due to the immense engine exhaust flames they trailed—enabling us to sight them from long range—we enjoyed a great advantage over these bombers. The chief disadvantage lay in their low speed—barely 180 kph—rendering an attack from astern virtually impossible. The only way to bring them down was from the flanks. Our He 111 had been fitted out in Wiener-Neustadt with five 2-cm cannon. They were utilized on this sortie to bring down the *Viermots*. I maneuvered myself side-on to and some distance ahead of the Russians and simply let them fly through the sights. All three machines were instantly set alight, ablaze from starboard to port wingtip. We returned to Orsha in the dark to replenish our munitions for a second sortie, which as luck would have it, could not be flown. We had in the interim received orders to move to Neuburg-Donau, where we were to be reequipped with the Ju 88 mounting oblique weapons, the so-called *Schräge Musik*. My Staffel moved by rail in September 1943, leaving our He 111s in Orsha.

## In Profile:
# Ju 88 C-6 "C9+AE", IV./NJG 5

Ju 88 C-6 coded "C9+AE" was one of two Ju 88 C-6s flown by Hptm. zu Sayn-Wittgenstein in IV/NJG 5 on the Eastern Front. Equipped with FuG 212 radar, the lower fuselage *Bodenwanne* gondola and *Schräge Musik* mounted in line astern, "C9+AE" may well have been one of the first Ju 88s so equipped. His second C-6 coded "C9+DE" lacked all these features and was apparently flown on clear, bright nights as an *Expreßjäger* or "fast-hunter." Wittgenstein scored most of his victories over Kursk in this machine. "C9+AE" displays a yellow fuselage Eastern theatre band, black lower surfaces, and mottled dark gray finish (probably 74/75).

Bf 110 crews from the Zestörergeschwader with blind-flying skills were also organized into ad hoc night fighter units. These units included 10.(N)/ZG 1, where the young Ofw. Josef Kociok, previously with ZG 76 and SKG 210, was to make a name for himself, being credited with 16 Soviet aircraft shot down at night between February and July 1943. The Bf 110s went out at night to track down Soviet aircraft bombing the front line or supplying partisans. If necessary, these aircraft would attack partisan camps behind German lines. On the night of September 26/27, Kociok scored his 21st night victory downing a DB-3 but, with his crewman, had to abandon his damaged Bf 110 G. His parachute failed to deploy, and he perished, while his gunner/radio operator escaped unscathed. With 33 victories in the East, Kociok was posthumously promoted to Leutnant.

In April 1943, part of NJG 5 was detached for a short time to East Prussia where its Kommodore, Hptm. zu Sayn-Wittgenstein, was virtually the only pilot to achieve anything of note by scoring three victories over DB-3 bombers. In July, in preparation for Operation *Zitadelle* (the Kursk offensive), the Stab, 10. and 12./NJG 5 were deployed to Orel. On the 16th, a 12. Staffel Do 217 J crashed at Orel and, on the 19th, a Ju 88 C-6 of 10./NJG 5 was destroyed at Bryansk. The first two combat losses occurred on August 7, when one aircraft from each Staffel was shot down. Once again, zu Sayn took the lion's share, being credited with 29 Soviet aircraft between July 14 and August 8. Another meteoric ace was Oblt. Robert Landau (10./NJG 5) who scored five victories in July but was killed on the night of July 19/20 in a crash-landing at Bryansk after downing a DB-3 bomber.

With the situation in the East becoming tense after Stalingrad and Kursk, the Luftwaffe command was forced to create new night fighter units in the East. A new night-fighting Geschwader emerged in early August—NJG 100. I. Gruppe came into being at Bryansk. This

The aircraft of Oblt. Martin Bauer, Staka of 11./NJG 6, at Otopeni. The aircraft displays the *Englandblitz* emblem and the pilot's personal insignia.

was only a partial redesignation, with Stab IV./NJG 5 becoming Stab/NJG 100. Wittgenstein led the unit for only a short while, however, before leaving to command II./NJG 3 and handing over to Maj. Rudolf Schoenert. 12./NJG 5 formed 1./NJG 100. 10. and 12./ZG 1 gave up crews to form 3. Staffel. 2./NJG 100 was then likely made up of a wide variety of crews.

The formation of NJG 200 on August 17 was even more absurd as this Geschwader never had a Stab … far less a full complement. 1./NJG 200 was the redesignation of the Nachtjagdschwarm of Luftflotte 1 at Dno; 4./NJG 200 was formed at Orscha from the remnants of 10./ZG 1; 5./NJG 200 at Nikolajew was the former NJ *Schwarm* of Luftflotte 4, while 7./NJG 200 came from the NJ *Schwarm* of Luftflotte 6 at Smolensk. 7./NJG 200 was disbanded in December. On the same date, an 8./NJG 200 was established at Stalino with a combination of He 111s, Ju 88As, and Fw 190s. Given the lack of success of this disparate Staffel, it moved to Neuburg in October to be reequipped with Ju 88 Cs.

A partial organization chart dated August 31 lists the strength of the Nachtjagd in the USSR:

II./NJG 200: 21 Bf 110s (13 serviceable) (Lfl 4); I./NJG 100: 40 (27) Bf 110s, Do 217s, and Ju 88s (LFl 6); 8/NJG 100: six (six) He 111s, Ju 88s, and Fw 190s (Lfl 6); 1/NJG 200: eight (four) Bf 110s and Ju 88 (Lfl 1). For a total of just 75 rather disparate aircraft, around 50 were combat-ready.

Documentation for these units is meager. For 1943, there is only one victory by 1./NJG 100 (a "Mitchell") and a dozen others credited to 2./NJG 100 (R-5 and PS-84), including four by Hptm. Henrik von Hemskerck, a former Staka of 10./KG 26 who switched to night

Eastern Front ace Ofw. Josef Kociok was killed in action on the night of September 26/27, 1943.

fighting in 1942. Evidently there were far more claims than this, as Maj. Alois Lechner (1./NJG 100) is said to have obtained 10 *Luftsiege* in August 1943 alone. In December, 2./NJG 100 moved to Focsani in Romania to operate with IV./NJG 6. This Staffel had at its disposal a train and wagons which served as crew accommodation, and which also hauled a Freya and two Würzburgs to guide the Ju 88s.

In Romania, IV./NJG 6, established to defend the oilfields, faced little opposition at the time, while training a dozen Romanian crews on Bf 110s in the first night fighter unit of the Royal Romanian Air Force. As the Gruppe only comprised two Staffeln, 10 and 11, the Romanian squadron was more or less officially designated 12./NJG 6. On August 1, however, a large force of USAAF B-24s from Africa raided the Ploesti refineries—Operation *Tidal Wave*. With only one day fighter Gruppe available, 10. and 12./NJG 6 were also scrambled and, in the course of these battles, two Liberators were downed for the loss of two Bf 110s (including the crew of the Romanian squadron leader, Capitan Marin Ghica).

It was probably because of this attack that the Luftwaffe command accelerated the dispatch of a composite night fighter Staffel to Mizil. 10./JG 301 was intended to reinforce IV./NJG 6, but it was cobbled together, with pilots from disparate backgrounds—Fw. Karl Unger had been a school instructor, Fw. Walter Waldenberger had been a Ju 52 pilot with KGzbV 1, while Ofw. Egon Gerz came from an *Überführungs* (ferry) unit. While all these airmen undeniably had some flying experience and were competent blind flyers, they had little combat training.

On September 14, Fw. Karl Gunselmann (11./NJG 6) scored the Gruppe's first victory when he shot down a DB-3 on a mine-laying sortie over the Danube.

Although encounters with the enemy were rare, IV./NJG 6 suffered losses due to poor aircraft maintenance and lack of infrastructure on the Romanian airfields.

A lineup of *Wilde Sau* Bf 109 Gustavs assigned to 10./JG 301 at Ploesti, Romania. The aircraft wear a very light-colored night fighter finish and feature a narrow yellow fuselage band. The JG 301 pilot in the shot is Oblt. Alexander "Axel" Graf Rességuier de Miremont, an original member of JG Herrmann.

# In Profile:
# Engelbert Heiner

The complications of the so-called Nachtjagd Ost (East) are illustrated by the career of Oblt. Engelbert Heiner. Born in Krefeld in 1914, he joined the Luftwaffe in 1935 and, as a member of KG 157, took part in the Spanish Civil War in 1938 as a bomber pilot with the Condor Legion. Transferred to 9./KG 27, he fought in Poland. During the *Westfeldzug*, he came down on May 14, 1940, near Louvain, but returned to his unit. On May 19, 1940, he was shot down by French fighters near Epinal and captured. Escaping captivity nine days later, he fought over England and then in the USSR. In late 1941 he was General Kurt Pflugbeil's personal pilot (4. Fliegerkorps) for six months. In 1942, he returned to his Staffel and fought over Sevastopol. Skilled on instruments, he was one of a handful of pilots from 9./KG 27 who made up the Nachtjagdschwarm of Luftflotte 4. On August 10/11, 1942, during a night mission, his He 111 was shot down near Woronesch, but he was able to bail out. Having scored 11 night victories in the He 111, he was awarded the Ritterkreuz on December 9, 1942, and became an instructor with IV./KG 27. With bomber units disbanded at the end of 1944, Heiner was retrained as a night fighter and, in December 1944, became Staka with 10./NJG 6. In February 1945, he scored some five unconfirmed victories but was shot down and killed near Gelnhausen on the night of March 18/19 by a 157 Sqn Mosquito.

An excellent night fighter ... albeit at the controls of He 111. Engelbert Heiner was KIA near the end of the war. Note his RK has been "censored" from this image.

## In Profile:
## Bf 110 G "2N+GU", 5./NJG 200

Ofw. Josef Kociok's 10.(NJ)/ZG 1 Bf 110 G coded "2N+GU"—the "G" is repeated on the nose below the cockpit air intake. With his BF Fw. Alexander Wegerhoff, Kociok scored multiple kills in the East during the summer of 1943 and was awarded the RK for 27 victories (15 by night) on July 31, 1943. 10. (NJ)/ ZG 1 was redesignated 5./ NJG 200 during August 1943. Kociok was KIA during the night of September 26/27, 1943, after colliding with a Soviet bomber he was attempting to bring down. Both Kociok and Wegerhoff bailed out from Bf 110 G-2 WNr. 6392—Kociok's chute failed to open. Kociok tallied some 33 victories in the East in some combat sorties.

# In the West: August–December 1943

The final raid of Operation *Gomorrah*—the assault on Hamburg—took place on the night of August 2/3, 1943. During an attack by 740 RAF "heavies," the Nachtjagd downed 19, victories won mainly by aces like Maj. Radusch (two v.), Hptm. Schoenert, and Hptm. Jabs. The single-engine fighters of JG Herrmann achieved four *Luftsiege*. Two II./NJG 3 Do 217s were lost in combat. One of them was flown by Hptm. Hans Baer, ex-Staka of 12.(N)/JG 2 and 4./NJG 3. After convalescing, he became Kommandeur of II./NJG 5 but died on December 20/21, 1943.

May 1940 in Vaernes. Three IV.(N)/JG 2 officers enjoying the sunshine. From left: Lt. Jürgen Waldhelm (Staka of 11.(N)/JG 2), Lt. Damman, and Oblt. Hans Baer (Staka of 12.(N)/JG 2). Baer was to lead 4./NJG 3 (but was wounded in August 1943) then II./NJG 5 before being killed in an accident with eight victories to his name. Waldhelm, a Staka with 5./NJG 1, switched to day fighting (6./JG 3) and then went to the Schlacht arm. As Staka of 1./Schl.G. 2, he was killed in Russia on January 7, 1943.

Four pilots were honored on August 2: Maj. Helmut Lent was awarded the Schwerter for his 65 night victories and was appointed Kommodore of NJG 3; Hptm. Egmont Prinz zur Lippe-Weißenfeld (Kdr of III./NJG 1) was awarded the Eichenlaub after 45 victories; Hptm. Manfred Meurer (Staka 3./NJG 1), who had just returned his 50th *Abschuss*, also received the Eichenlaub. Shortly afterward, he was posted to take charge of II./NJG 5; and Oblt. Rudolf Sigmund (Staka of 10./NJG 1) was awarded the Ritterkreuz for 26 victories (including a B-17 and a B-24 by day) and was promoted Kommandeur of III./NJG 3.

In early August, Bomber Command raided Milan and Turin, crossing French airspace, which was largely devoid of antiaircraft defenses. Nevertheless, Hptm. Hans-Wolfgang von Niebelschütz (5./NJG 4) won victories on the nights of August 7/8, August 12/13, and August 14/15. When it became apparent that the RAF could violate French airspace with virtual impunity, Fw 190s from JG 2 flown by pilots trained on instruments, were deployed. On the night of August 15/16, 2./JG 2 shot down seven four-engine aircraft and two more the following night. However, these were only "one-offs."

In August 1943, Bomber Command launched several attacks against northern Italy. On the evening of the 16th, four Bf 110s from 2./NJG 4 departed Florennes to intercept the stream heading southward. According to the account of 2./NJG 4 gunner, Uffz. Werner Uhlmann:

Hptm. Hans von Niebelschütz, a former long-distance reconnaissance pilot in 4.(F)/121, transferred to the Nachtjagd (NJG 4 then NJG 5) as did other instrument-trained aviators. He scored eight victories before falling victim to Flak in January 1944.

At Laon, a Ju 88 C-6 of I./NJG 4 displays a shark's mouth (*Haifischmaul*) which was probably painted out because it was too visible at night.

Photo published in the *Illustrierter Beobachter*: Hermann Göring receives four aces decorated on August 2, 1943. From left: Hptm. Egmont zur Lippe-Weißenfeld (Kdr of III./NJG 1), Maj. Helmut Lent (who was to lead NJG 3), Maj. Hajo Herrmann (instigator of the *Wilde Sau*) and Hptm. Manfred Meurer (who was to lead II./NJG 5). All four Nachtjagd aces were killed in action.

We took off from Florennes at 23.18. My pilot was Lt. Wilhelm Schneidewind, who had already scored two victories. He was older than me and had taken courses at the Napola. After more than an hour in the air, we were flying over the Beauce region when we were surprised by an enemy night fighter and took hits. Schneidewind gave the order to bail out. I tried to push the canopy open but the slipstream made it impossible to budge. I finally managed to lift it, but, as I jumped, my head slammed into the framing. My right leg was trapped between the folding hood and the rear cockpit armored plate. I struggled desperately to get free before I fell clear at around 7,000 meters. I was only semi-conscious when I hit the ground. Hard. I was lying in a field of beetroot. I realized that I was unable to move or get up and thought to my horror that I was probably paralyzed. I started shouting for help as loud as I could. That's how I attracted the attention of the locals.

Uhlmann had come down southeast of the village of Châtillon-le Roi. Four villagers heard the shouts and braved the curfew to come to the aid of the injured airman. His comrade, radio operator Mehnert, who had a broken leg, was also rescued, while the pilot's body was found with his parachute unopened. Mehnert recovered quickly and returned to Florennes. Uhlmann, who sustained compressed vertebrae in the hard landing, subsequently lost all his hair. After around 20 weeks in hospital, followed by a period of leave, he returned to Florennes and was back in action in June 1944. Uhlmann's "3C+CK" was downed by a 141 Sqn Beaufighter VIf flown by F/Lt. Kelsey. Uhlmann survived the war and returned to Châtillon-le-Roi in 1991 to thank those who had helped him.

During August, Bomber Command continued its raids on German cities in the face of a Nachtjagd arm badly shaken by *Gomorrah*. On the night of August 9/10, 457 bombers heading for Mannheim lost only 10 machines, six of which fell victim to night fighters. There were three victories for the new Gruppe, I./NJG 6, established by a simple rebranding of IV./NJG 4 from Mainz-Finthen.

On August 10/11, Nuremberg suffered heavy damage, but the Nachtjagd was only able to shoot down a dozen of the 633 attackers. On 17 August USAAF bombers mounted an ambitious raid on Schweinfurt and Regensburg, a twin-pronged attack designed to overwhelm the Tagjagd.

Uffz. Werner Uhlmann after his convalescence in 1944. Following his bail-out, he suffered from alopecia (hair loss).

The Luftwaffe launched virtually every serviceable fighter to counter the U.S. Eighth Air Force—including the Bf 110 Nachtjäger of which around 100 could be deployed by day. Obviously, the crews had only limited experience in this form of combat. Nine B-17s were credited to them for the loss of eight Bf 110s and nine airmen killed. The "lumbering" Messerschmitt twin was no match for the more agile American escorts. 2./NJG 4 pilot Norbert Pietrek recalled:

> That afternoon—August 17, 1943—we were ordered up to intercept American bomber formations. We night fighters considered this almost suicidal as the Bf 110 could not hope to match the American and British escort fighters. I took off from Florennes together with six comrades, among them Staffelkapitän Altendorf and my Katschmarek Gralmann, heading north. I'm sure Kowalzik and Schulenburg were also with us. But we were intercepted by enemy fighters and we immediately formed a defensive circle. However, Kowalzik stupidly left the formation to dive on a lone Spitfire [sic] and that let the enemy fighters in. Both Gralmann's engines were on fire, but he still managed to pull up his nose to get off a salvo that brought down one of the American fighters before bailing out and jumping clear.

2./NJG 4 had not run into Spitfires—their adversaries that day were probably P-47 Thunderbolts of 63 Fighter Squadron/56th FG. 1Lt. Edgard D. Whitley claimed a Bf 110, 1Lt. Glen D. Schiltz Jr. and 2Lt. John H. Truluck each reported having "damaged an Me 210." The dogfight, according to American reports, occurred between Ans and Sint-Niklaas at around 16.25–16.40 (BST). Two of the damaged Messerschmitts managed to escape by putting down at Sint-Denijs-Westrem airfield. Staka Altendorf and his BF, Fw. Wilfried Arndt, were less fortunate. Their Bf 110 (WNr. 6160 coded "3C+DK") became uncontrollable, and both bailed out near Assenede. The Staffelkapitän landed safely and his "sparker" Arndt was slightly injured. Pietrek continued:

> I managed to find shelter in the clouds and when I emerged I glimpsed the coast of England. I could see the condensation trails of B-17s returning from the raid. I closed on a B-17 and brought it down, watched it plunge into the sea, but in the absence of a witness, this was a victory that would never be credited. Our Staffel lost three aircraft that day …

Lt. Norbert Pietrek at the controls of his Bf 110 coded "3C+HK" in Florennes.

# In Profile:
# Oberleutnant Rudolf Altendorf

Rudi Altendorf was a successful *Zerstörer* pilot, returning four victories before his transfer to the Nachtjagd. As Staffelkapitän in 2./NJG 3, he was credited with the first NJ *Abschuss* on the Eastern Front, a Soviet bomber downed on the eastern approaches to Berlin on the night of October 20/21, 1941. Promoted to Oblt. he transferred to I./NJG 4 based in Laon-Athies, France, in the summer of 1942. I./NJG 4 moved in March/April 1943 to their newly constructed *Fliegerhorst* at Florennes and Altendorf was appointed Staka of 2./NJG 4. Flying a patrol in Raum 7 in his Bf 110 coded "3C+EK" on the night of July 13/14 Altendorf claimed two 102 Sqn Halifaxes south of Mauberge, including Halifax JD 297 which went down at 02:19. Remarkably, JD 297 was also claimed some 10 minutes later by Oblt. Ludwig Meister—both aces were subsequently credited with a confirmed victory. After the summer of 1943 Altendorf and his Staffel were transferred to Germany, where 2./NJG 4 became 12./NJG 5. On January 1, 1944, Altendorf was promoted to Hptm. and appointed Kommandeur of IV./ NJG 5 stationed at Brandis, where he achieved two further Ostfront *Abschüsse*. Altendorf survived the war with a total score of 25 victories, for which he was awarded the Deutsches Kreuz in Gold.

Seen left, Oblt. Altendorf was Staffelkapitän 2./NJG 4 during the summer of 1943.

Keeping up the pressure on the Luftwaffe leadership, 600 bombers set out for the rocket development and testing complex at Peenemünde later that night, August 10/11. A diversionary raid was launched over Berlin with Mosquitos. Around 40 four-engine bombers were lost, 42 of which were credited to the Nachtjagd (including two for JG Herrmann's TO Oblt. Friedrich-Karl Müller flying his usual Fw 190 "Green 3"). Only 19 were identified with any certainty, resulting in the first large-scale "overclaim," a phenomenon that was to multiply. Until then, confirmations had been precise, with each claim followed by a report—the first signs of a breakdown in the well-oiled machine that was the Luftwaffe.

Fw. Heinz Vinke (5./NJG 2) fell victim that night to RAF 141 Sqn Serrate-equipped Beaufighters off the coast of Borkum, under the command of W/C Bob Braham, patrolling off the northern Dutch coast on the RAF bombers' outbound leg. Serrate was a radar "detector"—homing in on the transmissions from the Lichtenstein, it turned the German hunters into "hunted." While the Bf 110 crews of Ofw. Scherfling and Lt. Grimm had already broken off the sortie due to engine problems, the Beaufighters intercepted Lt. Dittmann, Fw. Georg Kraft (14 victories), and Fw Vinke (at the time with 20 claims) out over the North Sea. Kraft and Vinke were both shot down by Braham. Vinke related an account of events to war reporter Walter Doelfs:

> I was airborne once again with my comrades on the evening of August 17, 1943. We were tasked with intercepting an incoming RAF bomber formation before they could reach the mainland. This meant that we were directed out over the North Sea and had soon left terra firma far behind. As we approached the first wave of bombers, one of my radar screens failed. As sure as damn it, I would have liked to stay with the bombers but had to make the very difficult decision to turn back. I could have screamed in anger and frustration. Suddenly my Bordmecaniker [flight engineer] shouted—"*Hinter uns ein Flugzeug*"—aircraft behind us! I immediately pulled our "Emil" into a tight turn, looking out for an aircraft but failing to see anything. Had he been mistaken? Unfortunately for us he had not. Suddenly there was an almighty bang and a fiery, crackling sound which took my breath away—*unsere gute "Emil" stand in Flammen*—our trusty Emil was ablaze! *Der verdamnte Tommy hat uns erwischt!* I tried to shout something out to my comrades but got no answer. The crew intercom had been knocked out. I attempted to put the Bf 110 into a turn, but the stick did not respond. We had to get out. It was agonizing not to be able to order my crew to jump clear. I just hoped that they had realized early enough what they now had to do. Our "Emil" had by now fallen away into a dive. With great speed and screaming engines, we plunged toward the sea. Then, with a loud bang, I heard the rear canopy roof fly off. I was relieved—the crew were getting out. Tense and thinking hard, I glanced at the altimeter, one of the few instruments on the panel that was still working. We were losing height rapidly, but I waited a few more moments until I felt that my crew had already left the machine. Then it was high time to bail out myself. With all my strength I managed to push myself up out of my seat and then the slipstream whipped me powerfully out of the cockpit, and I found myself spinning through the air. I pulled on the hand grip of the parachute, the chute rustling as it deployed. *Ein scharfer Ruck—und ich hing in den Gurten*—with a hard jerk I was hanging in the straps. I felt a wonderful feeling of happiness as I hung from the chute, gently swinging. Our mortally wounded aeroplane plummeted into the depths below me with a shrill, howling sound. Then it became completely silent. I shouted out the names of my

two crew—Fw. Schoedel and Uffz. Gaa—but waited in vain for any response. Only the rustling of the parachute silk could be heard. What had happened to them? Had they been able to get clear of the aircraft? I thought of them with an anxious heart. Then I hit the water.

In the end Vinke was adrift for 20 hours in his dinghy in the North Sea before being rescued. He was the only survivor of his crew.

There was a slight lull in the RAF raids. On August 20, Hajo Herrmann's single-engine unit was redesignated JG 300 with a Stab and a first Gruppe At the same time orders were issued for the establishment of a second *Wilde Sau* unit—JG 301—followed in November by a third, JG 302. Boosting JG Herrmann to Geschwader strength was only achieved by sharing aircraft—with II and III./JG 11. It was the same story for JG 301 and 302—lack of aircraft meant that only one Gruppe from each had its own fighters. The other Gruppen, so-called *Aufsitzer* or "piggyback" Gruppen, were forced to share the aircraft with day-fighter units. JG 300 and its sister units JG 301 and JG 302 were collectively brought together as 30 Jagddivision under Herrmann's command. Following their "success" over Peenemünde, JG 300 pilots shot down 13 RAF "heavies" on the night of August 23/24 as Berlin was raided by 710 Lancasters, Halifaxes, and Stirlings, of which 63 failed to return. Müller (Stab JG 300) and Lt. Robert Plewa of 2./JG 300 claimed triples.

On August 27/28, 674 bombers returned to Nuremberg, losing 33 of their number. The Nachtjagd was credited with 35 victories (seven to JG 300), of which 26 can be confirmed. On August 29, Maj. Günther Radusch leading II./NJG 3 was rewarded for his 37 victories with the Ritterkreuz. On August 30/31 Münchengladbach and Rheydt were the targets of 660 bombers—25 were lost, while the Nachtjagd was credited with 23 victories (21 would be confirmed). Given the location of the two towns JG 300 was not involved and it was mainly NJG 1 that distinguished itself in the sector.

By late August, Göring realized that his night fighters were struggling. Bomber Command was operating over German cities without sustaining the kinds of losses that might compromise the bombing offensive. Some 216 victories had been awarded to twin-engine and single-engine night fighters, but this figure was probably overinflated by as much as 30 percent. The Nachtjagd was also being worn down. In August, some 40 of its twins (Do 217s, Bf 110s) were lost in combat. Around 10 single-engine machines from JG 300 could be added to this total. Reinforcing the Nachtjagd was becoming a headache. At the beginning of August, IV./NJG 5 had moved east to become I./NJG 100 and was strengthened mostly with young crews. A new Gruppe, V./NJG 5, was created at Insterburg on August 11 under Kommandeur Hptm. Erhard Peters but with novice pilots supervised by veterans.

At the end of the month, three aces were honored: on August 29, Maj. Walter Ehle (Kdr II./NJG 1) was awarded the Ritterkreuz for his 34 victories. The same award was presented to Ofw. Walter Kollak (8./NJG 4) with 30 victories. On August 31, Hptm. Heinrich Prinz zu Sayn-Wittgenstein, recently appointed Kommandeur of II./NJG 3, was awarded the Eichenlaub for his 54 *Abschüsse* (many on the Eastern Front).

The beginning of September saw two attacks on Berlin: on the night of August 31/September 1, 622 bombers were effectively countered and lost 50 machines. Of these, 46 were attributed to the Nachtjagd (around 10 to JG 300); eight fighters were lost, including

Maj. Ehle is congratulated by Gen. Kammhuber while Ofw. Kollak awaits his turn to receive the Ritterkreuz.

that of Hptm. Wilhelm Telge (5./NJG 1), an ace from St.-Trond, who collided with a 460 Sqn Lancaster over Lückenwalde (see II./NJG 1 war diary extract on p. 31); on the night of September 3/4 braving the bad weather, 316 bombers lost just 20 aircraft while the Nachtjagd put up very little fight. The Nachtjagd were credited with 15 victories (around 10 in reality).

To reinforce the defense of Berlin, Nachtjäger detachments were called up to airfields near the capital. I./NJG 4 flew from Florennes to Stendal on September 5, then to Neuruppin on the 6th. The Gruppe reached Brandis on the 11th before returning to Belgium shortly afterward.

On the night of September 5/6, 605 RAF bombers targeted Mannheim and Ludwigshafen, with 34 failing to return. The Nachtjagd was credited with 38 victories. That night, Ritterkreuzträger Oblt. Heinz Strüning, leading 3./NJG 1, had to bail out of his He 219 A-0 over Jülich, his engines knocked out by enemy fire. His radio operator was killed. On the night of August 30/31, he had claimed three victories. Although wounded, Strüning returned to action.

On September 6, 9./NJG 101 was engaged by day against 262 B-17s attacking Stuttgart. It was awarded two Fortresses for no losses. On the night of September 6/7, 404 RAF bombers raided Munich. Seventeen were downed, 19 being credited to the Nachtjagd (including six to JG 300). By now, *Wilde Sau* successes were being impacted as weather conditions started to deteriorate with the end of summer. This loss of quality was compensated by the technical improvements made to the NJ twins, whose crews had gradually overcome the "trauma" of Window. The *Zahme Sau* or "tame boar" tactic saw night fighters sent to orbit radio beacons where numbers of machines could be stacked and progressively infiltrated into the bomber stream. This so-called *Einschleusung*, or guiding the fighters in, was starting to restore something of the defenders' effectiveness.

On September 15, NJG 6 was expanded. The first Gruppe was the renaming of IV./NJG 4. A Stab/NJG 6 was formed in Schleissheim (Maj. Fritz Schaffer). A II./NJG 6 (Maj. Rolf Leuchs) was raised in Neuburg before moving to Echterdingen. While Leuchs had flown with NJG 1 and had several victories to his credit, Schaffer had only led a Staffel in KG 2 and was mainly an organizer. Experienced fighters were in short supply in the Nachtjagd.

On September 22/23, Bomber Command returned to Hanover with 711 aircraft. German guidance was confused, and the RAF lost only 31 aircraft; however, 36 were claimed by the Nachtjagd, including 15 to JG 300 alone (nine single-engine fighters lost). To add to the confusion of that night, a second *Wilde Sau* Geschwader, JG 301 (officially formed on October 1), was thrown into the battle, losing six aircraft for two victories claimed by Ofw. Kurt Welter.

The following night, 628 British "heavies" were sent to Mannheim—32 were lost for 37 claims (14 from JG 300), including the first victory for Oblt. Gerhard Stamp, an 8./JG 300 pilot who had won the Ritterkreuz in July 1942 while flying the Ju 88 with the famed Helbig flyers, LG 1.

Hanover was attacked again on September 27/28 by 678 aircraft;—45 victories were claimed (around 15 by JG 300, 301 and 302), a figure corresponding roughly to the British losses of the night (without considering the Flak claims). The last attack of September took place on the night of 29th/30th over Bochum with 352 bombers. Only seven claims were made by the NJ, although six four-engine bombers were lost in combat.

During this period, Hermann Göring made many visits to motivate his Nachtjäger. Here he congratulates Fw. Heinz Vinke (5./NJG 2) on receiving his Ritterkreuz on September 19. Vinke was one of the most successful night fighter aces of the midwar period.

In September, a good 30 twin-engine Nachtjagd aircraft were lost in action, including two flown by Ritterkreuzträger: on the night of 27th/28th, Hptm. Hans-Dieter Frank, Kdr of I./NJG 1, coming into land his He 219 at Celle, collided with another night fighter. He attempted to bail out but failed to disconnect the lead from his flight helmet and crashed with his machine. With 55 night victories to his name, this former member of ZG 1 was promoted to Major and posthumously awarded the Eichenlaub; on September 29/30, the Bf 110 G-4 of the Staka of 7./NJG 1, Hptm. August Geiger, was attacked at Hardewijk by the Mosquito of ace Bob Braham of 141 Sqn. The crew bailed out but drowned in the Zuiderzee. Geiger, who had scored 54 victories, was also posthumously awarded the Eichenlaub. In addition to these 30 twin-engine aircraft, the *Wilde Sau* had been depleted by several dozen Fw 190s and Bf 109 Gs.

Created from scratch, JG 301 was officially established at Altenburg on October 1, 1943, although its single-engine fighters had already been in action for around 10 days. There were other moves during the month—I./NJG 2 moved to Greifswald while the Stab/NJG 101 went to Neuburg. 8./NJG 200 was recalled from Stalino to reequip with Ju 88 Cs and became 4./NJG 100 in December.

October 1943 was not a particularly good month for the Nachtjagd—only 171 bombers were claimed in the West and losses were high. The month got off to a bad start: on the night of October 1/2, during a raid on Hagen by some 250 Allied aircraft, only two were lost, none of them falling victim to the Nachtjagd.

On the night of October 2/3, distant Munich was targeted by 294 Lancasters, nine of which did not return. Nine victories were credited but four were doubtful. Three were claimed by JG 300 and three more by NJG 101, which was a training unit. On the night of October 3/4, 24 of the 540 bombers sent to Kassel were lost—18 were awarded to the Nachtjagd, which mourned the death of the recent Ritterkreuzträger and Kommandeur of III./NJG 3, Hptm. Rudolf Sigmund, whose Bf 110 G was shot down near Göttingen. He had 29 victories to his name. That same night, two notable aces, Oblt. Martin Drewes (11./NJG 1) and Hptm. Walter Milius (I./NJG 3) were injured while bailing out of their damaged fighters. Both were to return to combat. On October 4, several night fighters were engaged during the day against B-17s raiding the French airfield at St.-Dizier. They were credited with two Fortresses, one of which was allocated to the Staka of 11./NJG 101, Hptm. Franz Evers, the first of two *Abschüsse* for this Ritterkreuzträger, a former reconnaissance pilot.

Hptm. Franz Evers was awarded the Ritterkreuz in 1941 while flying with 3.(F)/121. In February 1943, he switched to night flying and took command of 11./NJG 101 before serving in various units (NJG 6, NJG 2, etc.). He ended the war at JG 7 with two victories.

The following night (4th/5th), 400 bombers attacked Frankfurt am Main. Bad weather hampered the Nachtjagd, which was credited with only 12 victories (the number of aircraft lost). On October 7/8, Stuttgart was targeted by 342 Lancasters. Only five victories were claimed. Among the German losses was Maj. Erich Simon leading IV./NJG 3, an ace with 10 victories. On the 8th, two B-24s were shot down by II./NJG 3 during an American daylight attack on Vegesack. On the night of the 8th/9th, two attacks on Hanover and Bremen were launched with around 500 bombers—33 were claimed by the NJ. Over Bremen, the aircraft of Lt. Heinz Grimm (IV./NJG 1), who had just returned his 27th victory (including one in daylight), was hit by a flak shell which killed his radio operator. It was the third time Grimm had had to abandon his aircraft in midair, but that night he was so badly burned that he died on the 13th. He was posthumously awarded the Ritterkreuz.

On the 9th, the Eighth Air Force sent its Fortresses over Poland and East Prussia. Aircraft from NJGs 2, 3, and 5 were used, with seven B-17s credited to them. On October 14, the Eighth Air Force returned to Schweinfurt (after the August 17 raid). Sixteen B-17s were credited to the NJGs. As experienced pilots were exempted from taking part in these very dangerous daytime missions, 11 novice crews won their first (and often only) victory that day. Two Bf 110s were lost to escort fighters. On the 18th/19th, 360 Lancasters returned to Hanover. The NJ was credited with 20 victories, though 18 four-engine planes were lost. On the night of the 20th/21st, Leipzig was targeted by 358 Lancasters; 16 were lost in action, 14 victories being conceded to the NJ.

Bomber Command's last major raid of October took place on the night of the 22nd/23rd, with 569 four-engine aircraft over Kassel—58 victories were claimed by several units (NJG 1, NJG 2, NJG 5, JG 300, JG 301, etc.), while the RAF lost around 50 aircraft (a rate close to 10 percent).

Overall, through October, around 36 Nachtjagd twins—Ju 88s, Bf 110s, and a few Me 210s and Do 217s—were lost in combat. According to figures compiled by T. Boiten, some 61 Luftwaffe night fighters were destroyed in the month, the 25 additional aircraft comprising

Maintenance on an NJG 3 Bf 110 at Lüneburg.

the Bf 109/Fw 190s of the *Wilde Sau*. As in September, the Luftwaffe mourned the loss of some fine pilots (including a Ritterkreuzträger), while its night fighters, despite the various overclaims, were failing to inflict the sorts of losses—around 10 percent—that would have slowed the assaults inexorably destroying German cities.

November operations began on the night of the 3rd/4th with an attack of 577 bombers on Düsseldorf. This time, the guidance system effectively directed the fighters by following the H2S emissions of the RAF bombers, which lost 24 of their number, 18 of which were attributed to the Nachtjagd. Hptm. Manfred Meurer (Stab I./NJG 1) scored his 60th victory. The following night, 20 Stirlings were sent "gardening" (mine-laying) in the Kattegat. They came up against 16 fighters from NJG 3. Although three 75 Sqn four-engine fighters were lost, the night fighters were credited with seven *Abschüsse*.

On November 11/12, 134 Halifaxes were dispatched to bomb Cannes with the aim of hindering maritime traffic to Italy. Although France was virtually devoid of night fighters, two RAF bombers did not return. The German fighter arm was credited with five victories, three being attributed to the Fw 190s of 2./JG engaged at night over Normandy. On November 13 and 16, Nachtjäger were engaged by day to counter USAAF B-17s but failed to perform. On the night of November 17/18, a small force was sent by Bomber Command to Ludwigshafen to test the H2S. Only one Lancaster was lost, the seventh bomber to fall to Fw. Günther Bahr (3./NJG 6), formerly of SKG 210 and a future Ritterkreuzträger. But no less than six Bf 110s were lost and 19 airmen killed (as well as two JG 300 aircraft). Among these was the Kommandeur of II./NJG 1, Maj. Walter Ehle. Returning to land in St.-Trond, he was caught out by the sudden extinguishing of the runway lights, probably misjudged his altitude and his Bf 110 G-4 hit the ground, killing its three occupants instantly.

Fw. Günther Bahr (3./NJG 6) flew the Bf 110 on the Eastern Front during 1941/42 before retraining as a night fighter in March 1942. He ended the war with 37 victories and the Ritterkreuz. He was one of the "intermediate" Nachtjagd aces (not too young, not too old) who had gained enough experience to survive the conflict.

# *Kriegstagebuch*—War Diary of II./NJG 1, August–December 1943

**Compiled by Horst Diener, translated by Neil Page**

The month of August 1943 brought the Gruppe a further 24 confirmed victories. During the night of August 24/25 a report of heavy enemy incursions resulted in 10 Bf 110s being scrambled. The expected formations failed to materialize. It turned out that a small group of Mosquitos en route to Berlin had released *Düppel* [German codename for chaff or "Window"] out over the sea, the returns from which replicated a large incoming formation on our radar screens. As a result of our modified night-hunting procedures, which had not gone unnoticed by the enemy, this "mock" maneuver was probably used to study the entire mission and the associated radio traffic. On the night of August 27/28 the enemy mounted a big raid on Nuremberg—11 of our machines were sent aloft on *Wilde Sau*, accounting for a Stirling heading toward the target and a further four *Viermots* downed over the city itself. On August 29 we received news of the award of the Ritterkreuz for Gruppenkommandeur Major Ehle. The presentation and celebrations took place on September 4, 1943, at St.-Trond in the presence of General der Flieger Kammhuber. On the same occasion, Ofw. Kollak—transferred to us from NJG 4—received the same award. On the night of August 30/31 16 Bf 110s were put into the air to intercept an RAF attack on Mönchen-Gladbach and five victories were scored. Shortly after getting airborne on a second sortie, flown using the *Himmelbett* procedure, the crew of Lt. Witzke, Uffz. Heise, and Fw. Wutz were killed when their machine crashed, although the cause is not known. The crew of Uffz. Zöller had to bail out near the town after being hit by antiaircraft fire. Zöller broke his leg. RAF intruders dropped time-delayed ordnance which continued to explode up to daybreak. No damage resulted.

The night of August 31/September 1, 1943 was not a happy start to the month, despite the participation in the defense of the Reich capital and the six successes achieved by the Gruppe. Hptm. Telge—who had returned from leave on the afternoon of August 31—did not miss the opportunity to take part in the mission to Berlin even though he was not back on the flight roster until the following day, September 1. As a replacement for his combat-tested BF, Uffz. Telsnig, who was not in quite as much of a hurry as his *Kutscher* ("coachman") to be there from his holiday, he took Oblt. Freymann with him as radio operator. Shortly after his first victory (timed at 00:55) he collided with a Short Stirling (a 460 Sqn Lancaster)—which suddenly appeared in front of him and which he could not avoid—his right wing hitting the bomber's tail unit. The Stirling went down with its bomb load. As a result of the damaged wing, the Bf 110 entered a spin. While Freymann with the force of desperation managed to escape the cockpit and bail out successfully, Hptm. Telge went down with his aircraft. In Telge, the Gruppe lost a dear comrade. His funeral took place in his hometown of Badeleben near Helmstedt. The Kommandeur did not miss the opportunity to personally deliver the funeral oration for this fearless and honorable knight ("*Ritter*"). It certainly was not easy for him to do so.

During the same night Lt. Henseler was attacked by an RAF "intruder" as he came into land at St.-Trond. Of his crew fortunately only Ofw. Luedecke received slight injuries. The crew of Lt. Hager/Uffz. v. Bergen achieved their first downing over Berlin and attacked a second enemy aircraft. As this first firing pass failed to bring down the bomber and Hager had used all his ammunition, the pilot positioned his aircraft to allow Bordfunker v. Bergen to fire up into the bomber, setting its starboard wing alight.

Also worthy of mention was the posting of the talented night fighter Oblt. Schnaufer and his BF Uffz. Rumpelhardt during August 1943 to IV./NJG 1 following his 21st victory. He replaced the Ritterkreuz holder and "boss" of 12. Staffel, Oblt. Linke, killed on May 14, 1943. It was with this Gruppe—which he led from April 1944—that Schnaufer achieved his greatest successes. Up to September 7, the Gruppe returned four more successes over Manheim and Munich before relocating to Langendiebach on September 9, 1943. After downing a Halifax on September 23, 1943, Lt. Hager was forced to bail out of his burning machine. His injuries kept him off the flight roster for a while. During an important RAF raid on Hanover during the night of September 27/28, the Gruppe managed to scramble seven aircraft, although no victories were returned. Staffelkapitän of 5./NJG 1 Hptm. Rupprecht and his BF Uffz. Vornhusen crashed to their deaths 20 kilometers northeast of Wunsdorf. On September 30, the Gruppe moved back to their old airfield at St.-Trond.

During the course of two day sorties flown on October 14 and 18, 1943, onboard Funker, Uffz. Staffa, claimed a Thunderbolt downed although this victory was not confirmed. The crews Uffz. Koch and Uffz. Schneider were both shot down, Schneider and Hübner met an airman's death (*den Fliegertod fanden*). On October 17, the crew Uffz. Geyer/Ogfr. Heil crashed on a training flight following pilot error. In mid-October the Kapitän of 4. Staffel, Hptm. Barte left the Gruppe, having been entrusted with the command of III./NJG 3. Oblt. Finster replaced him as Staffelkapitän.

From November 1943 combat sorties were flown with a three-man crew. It was the role of the third man or *Bordschütze* (gunner) to keep watch for enemy long-range night fighters and to draw attention to recognized enemy aircraft. In late October a detachment under Lt. Henseler was posted to Bonn-Hangelar. In the meantime, the onboard search radars (*Bordsuchgeräte*) were undergoing continuous improvement. The new Lichtenstein SN 2 (FuG 220) wide-angle search devices (*Weitwinkel Suchgeräte*) were gradually installed in the Bf 110. Operating on a lower frequency of 90 MHz that was far less susceptible to jamming, the FuG 220 required the much larger *Hirschgeweih* (stag's antlers) antennas. These featured just eight dipole elements and resembled an enlarged version of the individual *Matratze* masts of the earlier FuG 202.

During the night of November 3/4 the RAF flew a major raid on the cities of Cologne and Düsseldorf. To counter the attack the Gruppe was reinforced with six crews from III./NJG 1 and six crews from IV. Gruppe. Maj. Ehle, Hptm. v. Bonin, Lt. Fries, Lt. Henseler, Oblt. Finster, and Lt. Ernst each reported an *Abschuss*. November

1943 was a bad month for the Gruppe. On November 10 during a transfer flight from Deelen, the crew of Lt. Ernst/Uffz. Lüning hit the ground near Maastricht and crashed to their deaths. It was really bad luck for this young crew who had been so happy on scoring their first victory just a week earlier (on the night of November 4). On November 15, Uffz. Hoffmann crashed on the airfield on a training flight and was killed. However, the date November 17, 1943, will live on in the memories of the personnel of the Gruppe. At around 18:52, Maj. Ehle and his crew were the first to get airborne to intercept an RAF raid on Frankfurt am Main and Mannheim. He was followed shortly afterward by a further seven Bf 110s. The Gruppe enjoyed no successes on this *Feindflug*. However, Uffz. Schwanke crashed on landing in Limburg an der Lahn, turning his Bf 110 over, injuring both himself and his radio operator, while his gunner, Uffz. Hein, was killed. But Maj. Huchel—as writer of this KTB—had more tragic losses to record that night. At around 20:20, returning from Mannheim, Ritterkreuz holder and Kommandeur Maj. Ehle—with his crew Uffz. Derlitzki and Ofw. Leidenbach—crashed near Horpmael as they curved in on a landing approach, their Bf 110 G-4 "G9+AC" (WNr. 5575) coming down three kilometers east of Heors. All three men were killed. This was the heaviest loss the Gruppe had had to bear. Gruppenkommandeur since October 6, 1940, thanks to his flying experience, his flying skills and his soldierly virtues, Maj. Ehle had contributed immeasurably to the development of the night fighter arm. He was an enthusiastic aviator and an exemplary officer and comrade. Firmly guided by the Kommandeur, II. Gruppe had enjoyed great success. It was not only the Gruppe who mourned his loss, so did the entire Nachtjagd. The funeral was held on November 22, 1943, at the military cemetery of Schloss Bürresheim; the Kommodore of NJG 1, Maj. Streib, delivered the oration.

Returning to St.-Trond on November 17, 1943, Maj. Walter Ehle leading II./NJG 1 was killed in a crash. He was buried in St.-Trond with his crew.

# The Battle for Berlin: November 1943–March 1944

Between November 18, 1943 and March 25, 1944, Berlin was subjected to a series of 16 major raids. The defensive effort by the Nachtjagd during that period was hampered by the winter conditions. Three attacks on the capital of the Reich had already taken place in late August/early September, but the massive offensive at the end of 1943 was launched with the stated aim, according to Harris, of hastening the end of the war. During these four months, Berlin was not the only target—Bomber Command also attacked other major cities such as Stuttgart and Frankfurt am Main. On the night of November 18/19, 444 bombers flew to Berlin while 395 *Viermots* were sent to Ludwigshafen to split the defensive effort. The two formations lost nine and 23 bombers respectively. Some 20 victories were attributed to the Nachtjagd. Somewhat paradoxically, with only 2 percent losses, the cost for the Berlin raiders was comparatively light, while the aircraft attacking Ludwigshafen had flown part of the way over poorly defended French airspace. This did not bode well for the future.

On November 19/20, in a raid on Leverkusen, 10 of the 266 bombers engaged were destroyed. Four were attributed to the Nachtjagd, while the Flak defenses were slightly more effective. On November 22/23, 764 bombers took off for Berlin, the largest force ever deployed against that city. I./JG 302 claimed four of the approximately 30 bombers lost. But once again, it was Berlin's powerful antiaircraft defenses that filed the lion's share of victory claims.

The following night (November 23/24), Bomber Command lost 20 of 383 Lancasters over Berlin. Fourteen were credited to the Nachtjagd. Fw. Hannes Forke, radio operator for Oblt. Ludwig Meister leading 1./NJG 4 recalled:

> At 19:30 we take off from Florennes, heading for Berlin. We fly north until I register the first blips on my screen. Despite the heavy interference, I can pick up a return. At 1,000 meters range, Oblt. Meister recognizes an aircraft. It is below us. The searchlights illuminate the cloud cover, giving the effect of frosted glass where each plane stands out clearly. We close in on an approach. At a range of around 30 meters, the Oblt. opens fire. Suddenly, a violent shock, everything is red around us! One of our drop tanks is on fire. We manage to jettison it quickly. Three "Tommies" have bailed out and flash past very close to us. One tears off the antenna, the other damages the landing gear cover. But our plane is still holding its ground, the engines running normally. On the left engine, however, a strip of white light flutters and flaps in the slipstream. Gunner Toni Werzinski shouts: "Cut the port engine! Coolant leak." But it is only a ribbon of canvas from

a parachute that has caught up. A large cloud of smoke is now being emitted from the "Tommy." The enemy bomber explodes at 20:15. By the time we come in for a perfect landing at Brandis, we have been in the air for just over an hour. We write up our combat report straight away to prevent this victory from slipping through our fingers again. We are well looked after and spend the night there. At 11:00 on November 24, we are picked up by another Bf 110 because our "SJ" must go to the repair shop to have its combat "wounds" patched up.

Lancaster III (JB528/PM-Q) of No. 103 Squadron crashed at Grebs for Meister's 18th victory. To strengthen the defense of the capital, various crews like Meister's were apparently temporarily based at Berlin airfields while commuting to their home airfields as needed.

On November 25/26, Bomber Command committed 262 bombers to Frankfurt am Main. Only two were lost, being attributed to the Nachtjagd. On November 26/27, 443 Lancasters returned to Berlin with 178 bombers diverted to Stuttgart—29 four-engine

Crewed with Ludwig Meister straight out of flight school, Fw. Hannes Forke was, according to his "driver," extremely reliable and competent, despite having to wear glasses. During *Gomorrah*, he is said to have been one of the few to distinguish the four-engine aircraft "through" the interference of "Window" thanks to the slight oscillations of their wings.

aircraft were lost, 21 of which were claimed by the night fighters relying more and more on their aces. Maj. Wilhelm Herget (I./NJG 4) obtained three victories (48th–50th) and Oblt. Eckart Wilhem von Bonin (II./NJG 1) a further two (his 26th and 27th).

During November, the Nachtjagd was still apparently handicapped by the fallout from *Gomorrah*. Its successes were relatively poor while losses amounted to some 22 twin-engine Bf 110s and Ju 88 Cs as well as a Do 217, an outdated aircraft but still in service with II./NJG 101. To this figure, it was necessary to add the single-engine aircraft of JG 300 to 302.

On December 2/3, a raid of 458 bombers on Berlin was not "doubled" by a diversionary attack (except for a few Mosquitos sent to Bochum). Here, the bombing was not concentrated and the length of time spent over the target allowed the Nachtjagd to multiply its attacks. Around 40 bombers were lost, of which 25 were attributed to the Nachtjagd. Uffz. Hugo Fütscher (11./NJG 3) achieved his first victories (four *Abschüsse*—reduced to three—which constituted his only score) while Hptm. Paul Szameitat (II./NJG 3) was credited with three. Oblt. Paul Zorner (8./NJG 3) won his 14th and 15th victories, Maj. Wilhelm Herget (I./NJG 4) his 51st and 52nd, Maj. Helmut Lent (NJG 3) his 80th. In addition to Fütscher, nine pilots achieved their first success that night. The aircraft of the Kommodore of NJG 5, Obstlt. Günther Radusch was hit by Flak over Berlin, but he was nevertheless able to bail out with his crew (a loss not included in the official list).

On December 3/4, 527 aircraft apparently bound for Berlin attacked Leipzig, Mosquitos flying as a diversion over the capital—26 bombers were lost, around 20 being claimed by night fighters. If Hptm. Paul Szameitat (II./NJG 3) was credited with five victories (21st to 25th), only one fledgling night fighter opened his score that night. Szameitat was appointed Kommandeur of I./NJG 3 10 days later.

Bomber Command let 10 days pass. During this period, there were various skirmishes that gave some idea of the various tasks of the Nachtjagd: on the night of December 4/5, Fw. Karl Georg Pfeiffer (12./NJG 1) shot down a Stirling over the Netherlands; it was on a mine-laying sortie off the Friesland islands. On December 10/11, Uffz. Klaus Möller (12./NJG 3) scored his first victory, downing a Halifax dropping agents to the Danish Resistance. On December 12/13, Ritterkreuzträger Hptm. Manfred Meurer, Kommandeur of I./NJG 1, at the controls of a Ju 88 R2 specially prepared for this type of mission, shot down a Mosquito, his 61st victory. On December 10, Meurer's regular BF, Ofw. Gerhard Scheibe, was awarded the Ritterkreuz, the first radio operator/gunner to be so honored.

On December 10, 1943, Ofw. Gerhard Scheibe (I./NJG 1) was the first Nachtjagd radio gunner to receive the Ritterkreuz. Almost a month later (January 21/22, 1944), Scheibe was killed along with his pilot, Eichenlaubträger Manfred Meurer.

On the 13th, taking advantage of thick fog over northern Germany, the USAAF dispatched 649 bombers to Bremen and Kiel. The Nachtjagd put up 47 twins which were credited with three B-17s. Three Ju 88 Cs and a Bf 110 fell to the fighter escort. The Staka of 4./NJG 3, Oblt. Gerhard Raht, had to evacuate his Ju 88 C-6 over Itzehoe. He returned to combat and ended the war with the Ritterkreuz and 58 victories. On the 16th/17th, 483 Lancasters returned to Berlin in force. If some 25 bombers were shot down, 32 more crashed on the return leg home due to bad weather. The Nachtjagd is said to have lost three twins and three single-engine aircraft. Once again, the *Experten* did most of the scoring—Oblt. Schnaufer downing four (37th–40th) with his *Schräge Musik*, Maj. zur Lippe-Weißenfeld taking out two more (his 48th and 49th). Two crews won their first victory, Fw. Johannes Gajewski (8./NJG 2) and Oblt. Friedrich Berger (2./NJG 3) who became an ace but was KIA on July 26/27, 1944 at Salzburgen with the single-engine NJGr.10. Schnaufer's own account of his feat that night was published in issue 2/44 of *Pauke, Pauke—Nachrichtenblatt eines Jagdkorps*:

> *Ich zähle diesen Abend zu den eindrucksvollsten Erlebnissen meines Einsatzes in der Nachtjagd …* I consider that evening as one of the most impressive experiences of my night-fighting career, not just because of the four Lancasters shot down—that involved a lot of luck—but because I was able to take off and land again smoothly under the most difficult conditions. Our airfield at Leeuwarden was "socked in" under a thick shroud of fog and it wasn't much better anywhere else. *Aber der Tommy war gemeldet …* there had to be some possibility of getting to grips with the "Tommy." In our *Gefechtsstand*, Hptm. R.—whom we named "*Der Vater der Nachtjäger*"—said that we would be too late to catch the bombers when I announced that I was going up. The Bf 110 just didn't climb that quickly … The wheels of my Bf 110 had barely left the ground than we were in the "soup" at 20 meters altitude. What would happen—would it be solid all the way up at altitude, did we risk icing up? No, in the end we were pleasantly surprised. Engines purring, the aircraft climbed excellently, and we emerged from the fog just in time.

Schnaufer's BF Rumpelhardt had already established communication with the controller operating the box codenamed *Eisbar* and at around an altitude of 5,000 meters the star-spangled sky was as clear as glass. The crew quickly forgot their earlier anxiety.

> The engines were running smoothly, parachutes were checked and in order. We were still climbing when we saw the first opponent some distance above us. He was out in front—one of the Pathfinders. Right up to the last moment he failed to notice us, and I needed just a single burst to set him alight. Pieces of debris and sheet-metal engine cowling flashed past us. Suddenly there was a huge flash—the fire in his fuselage must have set off his bombs. By now we were well above him, but we were shaken by the blast. But that hardly bothered us—we watched the last parts of a bomber that had literally disintegrated cascading down like gold and silver rain drops.

The 38th and 39th were "routine" but four *Viermot Abschusse* in 40 minutes was an impressive performance. According to Rumpelhardt, Schnaufer's mastery of the aircraft and his superb flying skills came to the fore with the 40th. Schnaufer continued:

> *es war aber verdammt schwer mit diesem Burschen. Es war ein alter Hase …* it was damn hard with this fellow. He was an old hand. He was trying to slip through our box unseen and was flying the most amazing maneuvers in the process. He

had been alerted—it would have been impossible not to have seen the flaming wreckage of his comrades going down. Something like that can be seen over 100 kilometers away. Suddenly the huge shadow was very close above me. It was then that I made a stupid mistake that helped my adversary. In the heat of the moment, I let off a burst of fire far too early, enabling him to spot us prematurely. We were on the receiving end of a salvo of tracer fire, which flashed so close past you could hear the whistling sound. Not a pleasant sensation! *Nun gab es ein wilde Kurbelei*— now the *Viermot* entered a wild twisting, turning series of maneuvers. I chose my moment carefully and made sure my rounds hit home. He exploded in midair into three large sections. The fuselage with the bomb load plunged to the ground near the airfield—the hefty ensuing detonation blew out all the windowpanes nearby.

In the end Schnaufer's landing was almost routine and the one part of the sortie that he "was a little bit proud of." As for Rumpelhardt, "this experience was proof that Lady Luck must have been looking out for us."

On the night of December 20/21, 41 of the 650 four-engine aircraft flying to Frankfurt am Main did not return. Forty-nine victories were awarded to the Nachtjagd (eight pilots obtaining their first victory). Wilhelm Herget claimed eight victories (53rd–60th) in 45 minutes. On the night of the 23rd/24th, 16 of the force of 379 Lancasters that left for Berlin were lost. A similar number of victory credits were awarded to the Nachtjagd which itself lost seven twins and two single-engine aircraft.

## "*Kam Hochmut vor der Fall*"—Pride Came Before a Fall
### by Lt. Rolf Ebhardt—1./NJG 1

I became operational with 1./NJG 1 in October 1943 after I had completed my training. I was 20 years old and had about 300 hours of flying experience. I had flown several types of aircraft but not the Bf 110, the main night fighter flown by NJG 1.

At this stage of the war, the Allies were well on their way to gaining complete air superiority over Germany and the occupied countries. By night, the RAF flew huge area bombing raids, whereas during the day, the USAAF attacked strategic targets such as marshaling yards, airfields, factories, and oil refineries. To avoid the destruction of our machines on the ground, we often took off when an attack was anticipated. We flew to remote areas and loitered at 600 feet until the area was "clean" again, and then returned to base. This sortie was known as a *Blindschleiche* ["slow worm"]. We did this at 14:48 on December 13, 1943, and returned at 15:38 because our airfield [Twente] had not been attacked.

To fly a runway approach in the Bf 110 it was necessary to select flaps 20 degrees, reduce airspeed to approximately 110 mph, then lower the landing gear. There were two buttons on the instrument panel very close to each other which deployed and retracted the undercarriage; directly beneath these were two similar buttons for the flaps. What we never practiced during our training was landing in close formation with other aircraft, as it was strictly forbidden. In the operational units, however, it was quite common.

As we approached the airfield at Twente that day, I flew fairly close to my Staffelkapitän, concentrating on keeping my 110 in the correct position. When it was time to lower the flaps fully—at 150 feet as we crossed the airfield boundary—I pressed the button. The Staffelkapitän landed safely. Suddenly, a red flare shot up into the sky, a signal to go to full power and go around again! When I saw the flare, however, I thought of flying school and remembered the instruction, "landing in close formation, *streng verboten!*" This was permitted in operational units, so I saw no point in going around. I continued my approach and after a few seconds touched down. I literally slid to a standstill—I had landed flat on my belly! What had happened was this: I wasn't 100 percent at ease with all the levers and buttons in the Bf 110's cockpit and had pressed the wrong button. So instead of lowering the flaps, I had raised the landing gear! The controllers in the tower saw this and had immediately fired off the red flare.

When I reported the mishap to the Kommandeur in the ops room, he jumped up from his chair and shouted, "Why the hell did you do that! I'll get you a scooter for Christmas shall I, then you can roll around all over the airfield!"

All this took place in front of the radar girls in the operations room. Naturally, I was very embarrassed. In fact, I was wishing the ground would open and swallow me up! To add insult to injury, a piece of my starboard prop had broken off and struck my foot during the crash landing. So I had to stay in bed for two days and could only hobble around with a walking stick with my foot bandaged up. This was my fourth (and last) belly landing: two in an Arado 96 and one in a Do 217—all of them due to technical defects, I should add!

Ebhardt drew this cartoon on December 13, 1943—the fledgling Nachtjagd pilot is seen receiving a telling-off from his Kommandeur. Note that his foot is injured and bandaged. The crash-landed Bf 110 was coded "G9+DS."

Two photos of a 6./NJG 2 Ju 88 R equipped with FuG 220 Lichtenstein SN-2 radar at Kassel-Rothwesten. On the night of December 23/24, 1943, Lt. Erich Jung of 6./NJG 2 won the first of his 28–30 victories. He survived the war but received neither the Deutsches Kreuz in Gold nor the Ritterkreuz.

The last raid on Berlin in 1943 took place on December 29/30 with 457 Lancasters, 252 Halifaxes, and three Mosquitos. Because of the bad weather, British losses were again minimal, at 18 bombers (2.5 percent). Ten *Luftsiege* were credited to the Nachtjagd. Between December 1 and 29, the Nachtjagd lost 32 twins (Bf 110 and Ju 88 C) as well as several single-engine aircraft.

According to Boiten, the losses on this last raid brought total Bomber Command losses during 1943 to 2,225 missing on night operations plus a further 5,177 damaged. The Nachtjagd was credited with an estimated 1,818 aircraft destroyed in the West. This number is almost certainly an overestimate, as the Flak was particularly formidable around Berlin

December 30, 1943, Lt. Gottfried Kurzwernhart (9./NJG 4) downed a B-24 over northern France but was himself wounded.

and the Ruhr. In addition, 76 B-17s were shot down during the day, a figure that roughly corresponded with reality.

On December 30, Lt. Gottfried Kurzwernhart of 9./NJG 4 based at Juvincourt shot down a B-24 returning from Ludwigshafen near Charleville, his first (and only) victory. However, he and his crewman had to abandon their aircraft and were injured. In addition, I./NJG 4 in Florennes lost three aircraft near Nancy (one killed), Karlsruhe (one killed), and Kaiserslautern (one killed), all three of them to escorting P-47s. Hptm. Hubert Rauh, Staka of 3./NJG 4, bailed out of his Bf 110 G-4 and escaped unscathed, unlike his crewmate who went down with the aircraft. Rauh was one of the last two Nachtjagd pilots to receive the Ritterkreuz, in May 1945.

The report of Kurzwernhart's only victory. He left the front shortly afterward. He is typical of those many forgotten pilots eclipsed by the successes of the *Experten*.

# In Profile:
## Bf 110 G-4 "D5+AA," NJG 3

This Bf 110 G-4 "Chevron bar D5+AA" was flown by Maj. Helmut Lent, Kommodore of NJG 3, Stade, September 1943—a "lightened" machine minus radar and bulky antennae and armed with just four MGs. War reporter Werner Kark flew with Helmut Lent's crew for the ace's victories 85–86:

One week later we are over Schleswig-Holstein en route to Berlin. Kubisch guides us in toward a target masterfully—barely 30 minutes since getting airborne and the first enemy bomber goes down. The bursts of fire hit home so accurately that the Lancaster was flung to earth from its calm flight path like a blazing torch, as if hit by a giant fist. All on board must have been wiped out (*vernichtet*). We saw no parachutes. The winds at high altitude may have blown us off course as we then spent more than 30 minutes searching in vain before Kubisch brought us in behind another target. When Lent unleashed a burst that hit home, leaving a wide gash in the fuselage burning like a gaping wound, the uninjured British pilot retained enough nerve to embarrass us: he suddenly flew so slowly that we had trouble keeping him in sight. The Oberstleutnant reacted just as quickly—he cut the throttles and reduced our speed so rapidly that we were able to follow the enemy's trail, which was visible from a distance. Once again Lent maneuvered us into a firing position. For four minutes we trailed the wounded bomber out over the silent landscape. By now the bright fire had spread to the starboard wing and the bomber was gradually losing height, descending lower and lower. After six minutes it finally impacted the ground. "*Das war ein zäher Bursche … that was a tough one*," said the Kommodore.

On December 31, even though the Nachtjagd was struggling to cope with the enemy's numerical superiority, the high command was keen to highlight the courage of its crews by awarding three Ritterkreuz to outstanding airmen: the able Oblt. Heinz-Wolfgang Schnaufer, Staka of 12./NJG 1, was rewarded for his 42 victories; Ofw. Walter Kubisch, Lent's loyal partner since the beginning of the war, was the second Funker to receive the Ritterkreuz; the Kommandeur of I./NJG 6, Hptm. Heinrich Wohlers, also received the award for his 28 claims.

By late 1943, the hard-pressed Nachtjagd was scratching around for reinforcements. At the end of December, only one "new" unit could be raised—NJG 102. The Stab/NJG 102 was established in Kitzingen with Maj. Albert Blumensaat as Kommandeur. In 1940, he had led IV.(N)/JG 2 and then, for a few months, the NJ. Schule 1. He had very little combat experience. I./NJG 102, also in Kitzingen, was the redesignated IV./NJG 101, while II./NJG 102 in Echterdingen was the ex-III./NJG 101. A "new" III./NJG 101 was to be reestablished in 1944. Like NJG 101, NJG 102 was essentially a training unit. The hope was that more crews could be trained up to make up for increasing losses in the night fighter arm.

At the end of 1943, Oblt. Schnaufer was finally awarded the Ritterkreuz for his score of 42 victories. He is seen here in February 1944 with 47 *Luftsiege* on the tailfin of his aircraft. From left: Lt. Kurt Matzak, Lt. Heinz Rolland, Schnaufer, and Lt. Friedrich Potthast.

## Nachtjagd Unit Deployments, December 1943

| | | | |
|---|---|---|---|
| Stab/NJG 1 | Deelen then Bönninghardt | V./NJG 5 | Insterburg |
| I./NJG 1 | Venlo | Stab/NJG 6 | Schleissheim |
| II./NJG 1 | St.-Trond | I./NJG 6 | Mainz-Finthen |
| III./NJG 1 | Twente | II./NJG 6 | Stuttgart-Echterdingen |
| IV./NJG 1 | Leeuwarden | IV./NJG 6 + 10./JG 301 | Otopeni/Zilistea |
| Stab/NJG 2 | Parchim then Deelen | Stab/NJG 100 | Bryansk |
| I./NJG 2 | Kassel-Rothwesten | 1./NJG 100 | Bobruisk |
| II./NJG 2 | Parchim | 2./NJG 100 | Otopeni/Zilistea |
| III./NJG 2 | Schiphol, Neuruppin, Venlo | 3./NJG 100 | Orscha |
| Stab/NJG 3 | Stade | 4./NJG 100 | Orscha |
| I./NJG 3 | Vechta | Stab/NJG 101 | Neuburg then Ingolstadt |
| II./NJG 3 | Schleswig | I./NJG 101 | Ingolstadt-Manching |
| III./NJG 3 | Stade | II./NJG 101 | Lechfeld then Riem |
| IV./NJG 3 | Grove | Stab/NJG 102 | Kitzingen |
| Stab/NJG 4 | Metz | I./NJG 102 | Kitzingen |
| I./NJG 4 | Florennes | II./NJG 102 | Stuttgart-Echterdingen |
| II./NJG 4 | St.-Dizier | Stab/NJG 200 | Dno/Siwerskaja |
| III./NJG 4 | Juvincourt | 4./NJG 200 | Orscha |
| Stab/NJG 5 | Döberitz | 5./NJG 200 | Nikolajew |
| I./NJG 5 | Stendal | 7./NJG 200 | Smolensk (anti-partisan) |
| II./NJG 5 | Parchim | JG 300 | Hangelar, Rheinem, Wiesbaden |
| III./NJG 5 | Neuruppin | JG 301 | Schleissheim, Seyring, Zerbst |
| IV./NJG 5 | Brandis | JG 302 | Jüterbog, Ludwigslust |
| The *Wilde Sau* had some 94 machines on strength—of which 64 were operational | | | |

An unidentified NJ pilot preparing to board his Bf 110 for a day sortie.

1944 began with another attack on Berlin. Of the 421 Lancasters sent to the capital on the night of January 1/2, 1944, 28 did not return. There were six victories (69th–74th) for Hptm. zu Sayn-Wittgenstein (NJG 2) and four (20th–23rd) for Oblt. Ludwig Meister (1./NJG 4) described in his diary by his Funker Forke:

> I was just dozing off when we were all woken up at 2 am. The "Tommies" were en route for Berlin. As luck would have it, we were alerted too late to intercept them. But at about 4.30 am we were airborne again from Florennes as they were on their way back. We were flying in sector 7B. About five minutes later, we were at the right altitude to make first contact. This sortie was our first time with the new wide-angle detection device. It proved itself straight away. At 4,500 meters, I picked up the enemy. We approach the bird very slowly. We closed on him—a Lancaster. Oblt. Meister fired the first salvo into the rear of the aircraft. When it didn't catch fire, we fired a second. It then burst into flames and went down. In the clouds, you could clearly see it tumbling as it went down. Like the sails of a windmill, a shadow revolving on the illuminated clouds. It went down at 5.15 am.

Lancaster III GT-D of No. 156 Squadron crashed west of Binche.

> We had barely banked away when I detect another potential target on my screen approaching from head-on. At 2,000 meters, we curve into a turn. The enemy is accelerating so we gain on him only slowly. We get close to the "Tommy" and open up. The inner left engine catches alight. But the fire seems to go out. We lose him again and don't know what has happened to him.

It was 05:36 and this Lancaster was about to come down in the English Channel.

> We are now swimming in the middle of the stream. I spotted some prey, three or four at a time. A plane opened fire on us. But at 05:50, we were again in a firing position behind a "Tommy." It caught alight immediately and went down at 05:51.

The Lancaster fell four kilometers northwest of St.-Pol-sur-Mer (near Dunkirk).

> We're heading farther west. We're still picking up contacts. At around 06:00, we fired on a fourth "Tommy," whose fuselage and right wing were burning. Pieces of it burst into flames and then disappeared into the cloud layer below us. It's certain that he won't be able to get home! It's possible that he's already in the water as we flew west to the Kanal.

Meister's fourth victim was the third to go down in the Channel—three bombers that cannot therefore be identified with certainty.

> Now we fly home. The constant changes of heading and attitude have made me a little air sick. Shortly after 06:30 we come into land at Florennes. At the command post, we still must write up the reports. Then we have breakfast. Oblt. Meister and Funker Werszinski decide to drive straight to the site of the first crash that had just been discovered. I decide to go to bed, fall asleep and don't wake until 8:45 pm.

Several Nachtjäger were lost, including the aircraft of Hptm. Paul Szameitat, recently put in charge of I./NJG 3. His Ju 88 C-6 was damaged by a Lancaster. Attempting an emergency landing at Obernkirchen, the ace hit some trees and was killed with his two crewmembers. He was posthumously awarded the Ritterkreuz for his 29 victories (including a daytime B-17).

There was no respite for Berlin: on the night of January 2/3, 383 four-engine aircraft returned—27 bombers were lost, as were 16 twin-engine fighters from the Nachtjagd. At least two NJG 5 Bf 110s were hit by flak. The claims were confusing. Although 23 victories were conceded to the night fighters, several were subsequently annulled.

A remarkable image showing the so-called *Mattscheibe* over a suburb of Berlin—searchlights directed onto the base of the cloud deck forming a translucent "shroud" against which the enemy bombers were quite visible to night fighters. (via Permann)

1944 had opened in dramatic fashion for the Nachtjagd crews. And once again they found themselves committed on day sorties, despite growing losses, both of crew and aircraft. For example, on January 4, around 60 night fighters were engaged against B-17s bound for Kiel. One Fortress was reportedly shot down, but three Nachtjäger failed to return. The following day, during another attack on Kiel, three B-24s, one B-17, and one P-38 were shot down by the Nachtjäger. Even the veterans were now involved, as Hptm. Walter Borchers (NJG 5) earned his 20th *Luftsieg* over a Liberator, while Oblt. Martin Drewes (11./NJG 1) also downed a B-24, his 10th victory. Some 14 NJ twins were lost, including that of Hptm. Borchers, who bailed out over Schleswig-Holstein and was hospitalized for a time. Also that day, a Ju 88 C of 7./NJG 2 was shot down by a Typhoon during a test flight at Gilze-Rijen.

On the night of January 5/6, 1944, Bomber Command raided the distant port of Stettin. Sixteen of the 358 bombers were lost, 15 of them to 11 experienced pilots. One of them was Oblt. Paul Zorner, leading 8./NJG 3:

> The weather conditions were appalling. The cloud ceiling was relatively low, between 400 and 600 meters. It was also raining heavily. I switched on the SN-2 interception radar when my Funker Wilke patted me on the back and showed me four blue lights clearly indicating the engines of a heavy bomber heading for its target. Given the rain, I had to attack from the rear. I concentrated on his left wing and fired from 100 meters. A direct hit! Immediately, the plane disappeared vertically into the clouds. We then headed for the capital. My radio operator reported another contact. I saw a Lancaster flying in front of me but a little lower down. I immediately attacked, but this time I'd been spotted. The pilot launched an evasive maneuver and a machine-gunner caught us under fire. Surprised, I pressed the button on my weapons far too early and missed my target. I set off in pursuit of the plane, but every time I framed it in my sights, it escaped. I chose to approach from above and to the right so as not to lose it. I knew from experience that an aircraft painted blue like ours was hardly visible from this position. An opportunity presented itself. I was a 100 meters from him. I pulled back on the stick and opened fire. In a matter of seconds, my unfortunate adversary exploded, and his debris crashed to the ground at 03:51.

Zorner, at the limit of his endurance given the bomber's numerous evasive maneuvers, landed at Lüneburg. These were his 21st and 22nd confirmed victories. Zorner now had a highly sophisticated aircraft at his disposal, a Bf 110 G-4/R7: "The *Schräge Musik* was a remarkable weapon. You aimed using a special sight mounted in the roof of the canopy. But ideally, you needed a cloudless sky, a relatively rare situation." Maj. Werner Hoffmann, NJG 5, concurred:

> I got my first victory thanks to the nose-mounted guns, but from December 1943 I achieved most of my victories using *Schräge Musik*. I preferred it to the nose guns because it gave me a better guarantee of success. There was also a much smaller risk of being spotted and fired upon by the rear gunner. Our approach from the side and below, whether guided by our radar or from the ground, allowed us a better opportunity to spot the enemy against the lightness of the sky. At that point we could get under the bomber and match our speed to his and commence our attack from below.

On January 7, NJG 4 intercepted B-17s returning from Ludwigshafen and claimed two of them. The following day, there was another daylight battle with Fortresses operating over

On the night of January 21/22, 1944, the Nachtjagd suffered a grave loss with the death in action of Hptm. Heinrich Prinz zu Sayn-Wittgenstein, Kommodore of NJG 2.

Oschersleben and Halberstadt. The NJ claimed 13 B-17s, "for the loss of nine precious twins" (as T. Boiten pointed out). Braunschweig/Brunswick was the target on January 14/15, with 38 of the 406 bombers lost—41 victories were awarded to night fighters. Only two "new" pilots were credited with their first *Abschuss*.

On the night of January 20/21 the bombers returned to Berlin for the heaviest raid yet mounted on the capital. It was a clear night with good visibility. It is estimated that some 100 twin- and around 70 single-engine night fighters converged on the city—35 from a force of 769 aircraft were shot down by the Nachtjäger. Hptm. Autenrieth, Staka of 6./NJG 4 claimed a Halifax and a Lancaster, but hit by return fire from his second victim, he had to bail out and broke a leg as he slammed into the tail of his Bf 110.

On January 21/22, 648 bombers attacked Magdeburg, while around 30 aircraft were diverted to Berlin—62 losses were recorded in the Magdeburg formation and one from the Berlin force (i.e. almost 10 percent). Some 47 victories were attributed to the Nachtjagd. But that Friday was a black day for the Nachtjagd—the Luftwaffe mourned the loss of a talented Ritterkreuzträger crew, Hptm. Manfred Meurer/Ofw. Gerhard Scheibe of I./NJG 1. Their He 219 "G9+BB" was hit by debris from their second victim of the night, a Lancaster, near Magdeburg and came down barely 600 meters from their victim. The Eichenlaubträger Meurer had 63 victories.

At almost the same time the Nachtjagd sustained an even greater loss. Hptm. Heinrich zu Sayn-Wittgenstein, Kommodore of NJG 2, who had already claimed five successes that night, taking his scoreboard to 83 aircraft, was himself taken out by a Mosquito (probably from 141 Sqn). He apparently remained at the controls to allow his two crewmen to jump before perishing in his aircraft south of Lübars—although according to one source he never actually flew with a parachute. Posthumously, he was promoted to Major and awarded the Schwerter. As the leading *Experte* at the time, he was irreplaceable.

## *Luftkampfzeugenbericht*—Air Combat Witness Report
### Fw. Ostheimer NJG 2, Stendel den 23. Januar 1944

On January 21, 1944 I was airborne as Bordfunker with Major Prinz zu Sayn-Wittgenstein just before 21:00 on an operational night-fighter sortie (*Nachtjagdeinsatz*). The mission was flown under the *Zahme Sau* method in Ju 88 "R4+XM."

Just before 22:00 I had the first returns on my search radar. I relayed course corrections to the pilot and a little later we came upon the target—a Lancaster. We got into position and opened fire. The enemy aircraft's port wing was immediately set ablaze and the bomber started to go down at a moderate angle before entering a spin. The bomber hit the ground with a powerful explosion between 22:00 and 22:05. I witnessed the impact. We continued our hunt. I had returns from at least six other machines and with some changes of heading we came upon the next target, another Lancaster. After a burst of fire, we saw a few flames until the bomber tipped over its port wing and went straight down. Moments later I observed the fireball as the bomber impacted the ground. This happened at around 22:15. After the impact there were several other powerful explosions, no doubt the bomb load going off. Following another short approach, a third Lancaster was caught. A long burst of fire set it alight and it went down. I observed the impact at around 22:25–22:30. These timings are approximate. A short while later we saw another four-engine bomber. By now we were swimming in the so-called *Bomberstrom* [bomber stream]. This one too was attacked and went down trailing flames. I observed the impact at around 22:40. Again this is a rough timing, as all my notes were lost in the subsequent bail-out.

Once again, we soon had more blips on the screens. And following some adjustments to our heading, we came across another Lancaster. We closed in and attacked and soon observed flames in the fuselage, which became smaller as we looked on, so we set up for another attack. We were back in position and Maj. Wittgenstein was about to open fire when there was a terrible crashing sound and flashes in our aircraft. We were on fire. The port wing was alight and we started to go down. Then I saw the canopy roof fly off over my head and heard a cry over the intercom that sounded like "*Raus*—Get out!" I tore off my oxygen mask and flight helmet and was quickly catapulted out of the Junkers. After a few moments I opened my chute and some 15 minutes later landed safely somewhere near Schoenhausen. As far as I know we took a burst of fire from below, but I had no time to observe anything else. *Unser Absturz erfolgte kurz vor 23.00 Uhr*—our machine crashed shortly before 23:00.

Kurt Welter, a blind-flying instructor, volunteered for the *Wilde Sau* and was posted to 5./JG 301. Although the "wild boars" were reasonably successful during the summer nights of 1943, with the onset of fall and winter *Wilde Sau* operations became increasingly more demanding. The development of the Neptun AI radar series by Siemens was intended to go some way to alleviate the pilot's workload. Note the *Stachel* rod antennas of the FuG 217 Neptun in the rear fuselage of Welter's Fw 190 A-6.

On the 27th/28th, the 12th large-scale attack was mounted on Berlin with 515 bombers that lost 30 of their number—24 victories were awarded to night fighters. Although one pilot won his first *Abschuss* that night, young airmen added to their score: Uffz. Heinz Misch (9./NJG 2) won his second and third *Luftsiege*, as did Lt. Walter Kammerer (6./NJG 5), Lt. Spoden (5./NJG 5) his seventh and eighth. Misch would reach seven victories and survive the war. Kammerer would add an *Abschuss* to his list of victories before dying in March in combat with B-17s. The fate of the "young guns" therefore varied greatly. That night, Oblt. Baake (2./NJG 1) bailed out over Schleiden-Gemund after colliding with a Lancaster at 6,000 meters, his 24th kill. His radio operator, however, died.

On the 28th/29th, 67 Stirlings were sent to mine the port of Kiel, five hours ahead of a force of 677 aircraft destined for Berlin. Two Stirlings were lost on the early raid while 46 Lancasters/Halifaxes failed to return from Berlin. Some 40 of these were credited to the Nachtjäger. While Ofw. Heinz Vinke of 11./NJG 1 claimed three victories (his 42nd–44th), no fewer than seven pilots were credited with their first successes. For some, it would be their first and last.

A USAAF raid on Frankfurt was intercepted on January 29. Three young crews shot down a B-17, a P-38, and a P-47 but, once again, the consequences were heavy for the Nachtjagd, which lost seven Bf 110s (mainly from NJG 6). Another daylight battle took place on January 30, when 777 B-17/B-24s were engaged over Brunswick and Hanover. The losses

On January 30, Hptm. Friedrich Tober, formerly of II./ZG 26 and Staka of 8./NJG 2, force-landed his Ju 88 coded "R4+LS" at Wielen, one of the seven Ju 88s to fall victim to American fighters. Tober survived the war with four victories.

here were particularly heavy: four Bf 110s and seven Ju 88s, including the aircraft of the Kommandeur of I./NJG 2, Hptm. Albert Schulz, an ace with 10 victories (some credit him with his 11th on the day). Four B-17s and one P-47 were credited to the Nachtjäger. Oblt. Hermann Greiner (10./NJG 1), despite being an ace with 14 victories, was (exceptionally?) engaged during the day, being credited with a B-17.

The last raid of the month on Berlin took place on January 30/31 with 528 bombers, 33 of which were lost, while 34 Lancasters were confirmed to the Nachtjagd. Alongside the successes of the aces—Kraft, Radusch, Bahr, Schnaufer, etc.—two pilots scored their first victory and three others their second. JG 300 was not credited with a single success, but it should be noted that the Staka of 1./JG 300 was killed that night when his Bf 109 G-6 ran out of fuel. Lt. Otto Brüning was credited with 12 night victories.

January 1944 saw various movements and the formation of a new unit: IV./NJG 3 departed Grove for Westerland. 10./NJG 3 remained in Denmark to cover the North Sea and the approaches to northern Germany. II./NJG 4 temporarily left St.-Dizier for rest and refit at Fassberg before returning to France in February. At Werneuchen NJGr 10 was established, a composite single-engine fighter unit led by Maj. Rudolf Schoenert. It comprised three Staffeln; 1./NJGr 10 was based at Werneuchen with Fw 190s and Bf 109s, its pilots taken from the experienced crews of I./JG 300. Hangelar was its advanced airfield; 2./NJGr 10, at Werneuchen and Finow, was equipped with Bf 110s and Ju 88s; 3./NJGr 10 at Finsterwalde flew He 219s with, later, a few Ta 154s.

In February, Berlin was to suffer a single large-scale attack. During the first two weeks of the month, the Nachtjagd was only committed by day, achieving some paltry successes while suffering losses. On February 5, Hptm. Eckart-Wilhelm von Bonin, leading II./NJG 1, was awarded the Ritterkreuz for his 31 victories. On the 11th, Ofw. Hermann Sommer (3./

NJG 102), a veteran of the *Fernnachtjagd* (I./NJG 2) in 1941, was shot down and killed at Imsbach. At the time he was credited with 17 victories.

On the night of February 15/16, an imposing force of 891 bombers was launched against Berlin. This time, the fighters were ordered to attack only on the outward and return journeys, leaving the defense of the capital to the Flak. Some 48 four-engine RAF bombers were lost, 35 being attributed to the NJ. Oblt. Schnaufer won three victories (44th–46th) on his 22nd birthday and was promoted to Kommandeur of IV./NJG 1. Oblt. Wilhelm Johnen (5./NJG 5) was also credited with three *Abschüsse* (14th–16th). While there were no novice "firsts" that night, eight victorious "drivers" had yet to acquire ace status. So, as usual, the "hard work" fell on the established *Experten*: Greiner, Raht, Vinke, Augenstein. Eleven NJ twins were lost as well.

The night of February 19/20 marked the start of "Big Week," as the Western Allies launched a massive offensive against German industry in preparation for the landings in Europe. That night, Bomber Command launched no fewer than 832 bombers on the Leipzig aircraft factories. Losses were particularly heavy—82 aircraft—almost the 10 percent so feared by the British—77 victories were attributed to the Nachtjagd and, once again, the *Experten* took the lion's share. Fw. Rudolf Frank (3./NJG 3) shot down five Lancasters (31st–35th), Oblt. Paul Zorner (Staka of 8./NJG 3) four (27th–30th); Hptm. Erhard Peters, Staka of 9./NJG 3, was reported to have scored five victories (19th–24th) before being shot down and killed by a single-engine *Wilde Sau* (other sources give him "at least 12 victories"). Ludwig Meister, Staka of 1./NJG 4, recently promoted to Hauptmann, shot down two aircraft, as described by his "sparker" Hans Forke:

> The full moon period is ending and the moonless nights are coming, and so is the "Tommy." He's flying north. We set off, following the route of the incursions and, around Hanover, after about 90 minutes in the air, the first prey appeared on my screen. But nothing came of it. At around 2.40 am, I had another contact, and we spotted the "Tommy." It had a rectangular spotlight on its tail that blinded

During the attack on Berlin on February 19/20, one of the few "greenhorns" to emerge was Lt. Walter Briegleb of 10./NJG 3, who scored the first of his 14 victories. He is seen at Sylt in front of his Bf 110 G-4 between his mechanic/gunner, Ogfr. Walter Bräunlich (left) and his radio operator, Ogfr. Rudolf Brandt.

us. However, Hptm. Meister managed to close on him from the port side and get underneath him. I press the button [on the *Schräge Musik* slanting cannon] and it fires right between the two port engines. After a single burst, it crashed about four minutes later at 2.48 am [Halifax III NP-M of 158 Sqn fell at Breendenbostel]. At around 3.30 am, another return on the screen which led to an approach. This one caught alight in the same way between the two port engines. At 3.19 am, this "Tommy" went down. Other contacts were unsuccessful and, at 3.55 am, we land at Wesendorf. Thanks to their excellent coffee, we are in good shape and stay awake until dawn. Shortly after 7 am, we take off for Florennes. We were the only crew in the Gruppe to down any bombers that night.

On February 20, the Luftwaffe faced more than 1,000 American bombers. Four Bf 110s were lost, while three B-17s were claimed by the Nachtjagd. Oblt. Albert Walter of 1./NJG 6, an ace with nine victories, abandoned his aircraft with his crew. He immediately returned to combat but was killed on February 24. On the night of February 20/21, 509 four-engine planes bombed Stuttgart, losing nine of their own. Eight were credited to the Nachtjagd. Hptm. Meister again scored the only victory confirmed to I./NJG 4. According to Forke:

> We took off in the direction of Metz, the exact location was not specified. Shortly afterward, my screen picked up an isolated target at 5,000 meters. Little by little, we approached it unhindered. My "driver" slipped under the target and opened up, but it barely burned. He was twisting and turning, constantly changing heading. However, Hptm. Meister managed to get under it again and set it on fire. The enemy bomber burnt immediately, and we managed to pull away to the side. It fell like a stone [630 Sqn's Lancaster III LE-Q crashed at Plittersdorf at around 03:17].

A Ju 88 C-6 from 5./NJG 3 and a Bf 110 G-4 from 3./NJG 4 were lost. Although they were reported shot down in combat, according to the account of the Bf 110's radio operator, Uffz. Heinz Lhose, the only surviving member of his crew:

> The tragedy of the situation was that we were hit by our own antiaircraft fire and that it was the flight engineer's first and last night sortie. The left engine burst into flames and we couldn't get the fire under control; then the right engine gave up the ghost. The altimeter read 60 meters. I injured my head when I hit the aerial mast during the jump. My parachute deployed. I was very lucky. After a stay in hospital in Bad Schwalbach, I went back to work as a radio operator in Lt. Brünig's crew until the end of the war.

On February 22, during a daylight attack on the Danish airfield of Aalborg, Oblt. Hans-Hermann Müller, Staka of 11./NJG 3, shot down two B-17s (13th and 14th victories). During various daylight attacks on February 24, 10 B-17s were shot down (including four by inexperienced NJ pilots), for the loss of eight Bf 110s, one Ju 88 and an "old" Do 217 N from II./NJG 102. On February 24/25, two waves totaling 734 bombers attacked the Schweinfurt aircraft factories—34 were lost, 29 being claimed by the Nachtjagd—two falling to Hptm. von Bonin (31st and 32nd), two to Ofw. Kollak (33rd and 34th), five to Oblt. Zorner (31st–35th), etc. Five fledgling NJ pilots opened their score: Lt. Dieter Kehrberg (3./NJG 102) ended the war with three victories. Only four NJ twins were lost, including that of Oblt. Albert Walter (1./NJG 6), shot down only four days previously, who scored his 10th and last victory over a Halifax before being killed by a fighter at Egenhausen. That same night, Hptm. Lent shot down two Stirlings of 75 and 149 Sqns engaged in "gardening" (his 89th and 90th).

On February 25/26, the two-wave tactic was repeated to attack Augsburg with 594 bombers, 23 of which were lost. Three came down in France, victim of Hptm. Meister (his 30th–32nd). According to Hannes Forke:

> Our "SJ" was flown to Venlo to have the SN-2 installed. After landing, it made a good target in the middle of the runway and was riddled with bullets from enemy fighters. But that same night, we were able to take our revenge. We took Oberleutnant Thörl's "TJ." The Tommies flew to Abbeville and headed southeast. We were well guided. I picked up several prey and we quickly made contact. Hptm. Meister flew fantastically, positioned himself just behind a bomber and, with an accurate burst, set fire to the "bird," which fell at 8.55 pm [44 Sqn Lancaster III KM-A crashed at Berthancourt near Rethel]. By 8.59 pm, the second bomber had already been brought down. After the salvo, we didn't get out of the way immediately. The flames from the plane below us lit us up for a moment before it fell. Within a minute, it had smashed into the ground [Lancaster QR-K of 61 Sqn crashed at Menil-Annelles, southeast of Rethel]. At 9.05 pm, Hptm. Meister opened up on a third bomber. We were not close enough. Toni shouted a warning—a Halifax had curved in behind us. We quickly pressed the firing buttons and veered away. But the "bird" wasn't really burning yet. We kept a respectable distance. Then we saw a flash of light, the bright lights of incendiary bombs exploding. The aircraft jettisoned its cargo while continuing to burn and losing more and more altitude. I was amazed at how much cargo it dropped—the incendiary bombs go down considerable distances apart. Finally, at 2.14 am, this third bomber hit the ground [Lancaster I PH-P of 12 Sqn came down east of Laon]. The supplementary tanks didn't work, so we had to land. I couldn't get through to Florennes. Instead, I contacted Juvincourt where we landed. Our aircraft was replenished with ammunition and fuel. Toni carried out ground tests. When he reduced the speed of the engines, the intake pressure was too high and the left engine vibrated dangerously. No point in insisting, we had to stay on the ground! We find spartan accommodation in Cormicy … never again Juvincourt!

That night, five four-engine aircraft on a "gardening" mission over the Baltic did not return. Three were shot down by the Nachtjagd. Ten twin-engine planes were lost. The fighting of the previous night was to have a tragic outcome on the morning of February 26. At around 8.30 am, the Bf 110 G-4 of Fw. Heinz Vinke of 11./NJG 1 on an air–sea rescue mission off Dunkirk/Gravelines was intercepted by a pair of Typhoons from 198 Sqn. According to the ORB:

> 26th February. Broken loud cloud, fair vis. 2 Typhoons (F/Lt. Lallemant, F/O Hardy) were scrambled and vectored to Dunkirk where an Me 110 was sighted at 1,000 ft. Our aircraft closed and attacked. Head on and astern attacks put on the starboard of the E/A on fire, and further strikes on the cockpit caused the Me 110 to burst into flames and dive straight into the sea.

Vinke, a Ritterkreuzträger with 49 confirmed victories (and three awaiting confirmation), was killed with his crew. He was awarded a posthumous Eichenlaub and promoted to Ofw.

T. Boiten estimates the Nachtjagd score for the month of February 1944 at 178 bombers shot down by night and 19 American aircraft by day. I. Jagdkorps lost 53 aircraft in the process. The figure for the *Luftsiege*, still overestimated, could be reduced by at least 20 percent. German losses included those incurred in combat and during exercises, as well as aircraft strafed and bombed on airfields.

During February, the Stab/NJG 4 moved its HQ from Metz to Chenay, but this had no effect on its activities. On the 25th, II./NJG 4 left Fassberg and returned to St.-Dizier. Also in February, a "new" I./NJG 7 was set up in Münster-Handorf under Maj. Horst Bengsch, Kommandeur of III./KG 3. This was confirmation of the Nachtjagd's lack of manpower: the new Gruppe was a change of role for III./KG 3, which had competent blind-flying crews. This Gruppe, the only one of a "7th Night Fighter Wing," was equipped with Ju 88 Gs. As crews from III./KG 3 had previously facilitated Nachtjäger actions by dropping flares, I./NJG 7 continued these missions, being more of a support unit than a combat Gruppe.

On the night of March 1/2, 577 bombers attacked Stuttgart, losing only four aircraft. Five victories were awarded to the Nachtjagd, which lost two twins in accidents. A very poor performance. On March 3, in another daytime engagement, four NJ aircraft were lost and 10 others badly damaged, for a single victory over a B-17. That night a 199 Sqn Stirling on a mission to drop SOE agents was shot down at Echevannes (Dijon) by 5./NJG 4.

On March 6, during the first big daytime attack on Berlin, five B-17s were credited to the night fighters, two of them to Oblt. Hermann Greiner (18th and 19th). Two others were won by novices opening their scores—for Ofw. Fritz Rathkamp (6./NJG 5), it was his first and only success. He was killed three weeks later on takeoff from Stendal on a ferry flight, on March 28. On March 8, another daylight raid on Berlin took place. The night fighters were credited with a single B-17, the first victory for Lt. Rudolf Thun (6./NJG 5). Thun went on to achieve ace status with five victories, but was captured on May 2, 1945, shot down by ground fire while strafing an American column.

On the night of March 10/11, a 90 Sqn Stirling on a mission for the French Resistance fell victim to 4./NJG 4 near Brazey-en-Plaine. This upsurge in arms drops to partisans did not bode well for the Germans. On March 11, a veteran, Maj. Werner Streib, was awarded the Schwerter for his 67 victories. Shortly afterward, he handed over command of his NJG 1 to another old hand, Hptm. Hans-Joachim Jabs.

On March 15, Ritterkreuzträger and Kommodore of NJG 6, Maj. Heinrich Wohlers, an ace with 29 victories (five unconfirmed), crashed short of the runway attempting to land in bad weather at Echterdingen. Pilot and crew were killed. These were two more heavy losses for the Nachtjagd, which was gradually losing its *Experten* … and not just in combat. On March 15/16, no fewer than 847 bombers flew to Stuttgart. Although 37 did not return, 41 victories were awarded to the night fighters for the loss of 15 night fighters. A 6./NJG 6 Bf 110 G-4 coded "2Z+OP" got lost and landed at Dübendorf in Switzerland. The interned aircraft was studied by Swiss specialists, while the crew was sent back to Germany on May 22. Seven young pilots opened their scores that night, while Hptm. Meister scored his 33rd and 34th victories over France. According to his radio operator Forke:

> We are put on alert, another raid incoming. We take off. But the Tommies don't continue on the same heading. They turned toward Paris, then appeared to turn back. We did the same and landed without seeing any of them. We went back to our rooms. Then my *Kutscher* rings through to tell me that the Tommies have not gone home but have attacked Stuttgart. We get airborne again to intercept them on the way back. I wasn't expecting to go out again, but I was soon ready, while my pilot took a long time to say his goodbyes, which irritated me. Finally, we take off, but he hasn't closed his hatch properly, which flies open on takeoff. A false

On the night of March 15/16, 1944, Bf 110 G-4 "2Z+OP" of 6./NJG 6 landed at Dübendorf. The Swiss were particularly interested in the radar equipment, even if it was the FuG 202 and not the more advanced SN-2/FuG 220.

start and another return! Naturally, I grumbled! The Hptm. doesn't have a clear conscience and follows the heading I indicate without protest. We find ourselves in the bomber stream without any information. We had to turn 300°, since almost all the planes were behind us. At 0.56 am, my "driver" spots a target; we get as close as we can. At 0.58 am, we opened fire just below this aircraft. But the guns misfire and we don't know if the enemy catches fire. Suddenly, below us, an intense light! The bomber has exploded and by 1.00 am he was on the ground [Lancaster III HW-B of 100 Sqn crashed at Bonneuil-les-Eaux]. About 10 minutes later, I found a potential prey above us. We approached it quickly without being seen—in fact we only saw it when it was 100 meters from our cockpit. We opened up. The bomber caught alight but burned only slightly. Then the fire developed and, at 1.18 am, the plane impacted the ground to the southeast of numerous searchlights. We thought we were close to Paris [630 Sqn's Lancaster III LE-V exploded south of Besmé].

On March 18/19, 846 bombers set off for Frankfurt am Main, while around 100 aircraft on a "gardening" mission made a diversion over the Baltic, while 24 bombers from the main force were lost. The Nachtjagd claimed 20, a figure that was revised downward to 15. One single-engine and seven twin-engine fighters were shot down (including three Ju 88s by Mosquitos). On March 22/23, 816 aircraft returned to Frankfurt, while around 100 aircraft once again diverted to the North Sea and the Baltic. This would have divided the German forces. That night, 35 bombers were lost—42 victories were awarded to the night fighters, who lost eight aircraft. Hptm. Meister shot down a 514 Sqn Lancaster some 15 kilometers from St.-Omer, his 35th and penultimate victory. According to his own account:

The aircraft was repainted in Swiss colors. To avoid dismantling the equipment or risking a crash, a ramp was built to test the radar with the Bf 110 being overflown by Swiss aircraft.

We had landed at Hildesheim. My flight mechanic had spent the rest of the night readying the aircraft and hadn't had time to sleep. In the morning, we took off for Florennes. It was a joy ride—no threat of danger. My radio operator had contacted the flight control center in Brussels and they informed him that there were no enemy incursions ... Suddenly, near Namur, I felt impacts in the machine. I saw a plane sweep past. My mechanic hadn't reported it because he had dozed off. My engines lost all power. They hadn't caught fire but I was going to have to put down quickly. I dropped down very low looking for a gap in the woods to carry out an emergency landing. I removed my throat mike to avoid being throttled and managed to spot a flat area big enough to put down on. The plane slewed along the ground, both engines dug in, the tail came up and a huge cloud of dust and dirt billowed up. Ejected from the cockpit, I found myself lying on my parachute, my face covered in blood. I couldn't see a thing. I had splinters all over my face and nose and my hands were ruined.

As luck would have it, Meister had put down at Naninne near a rail track and help arrived quickly. Nevertheless, he was to remain in hospital for several months, not returning to his unit until late 1944. After the war, Meister was disappointed to learn that he had been the sole victory credited to P-47 pilot Captain Edward Sprietsma (367 FS/358 FG). An ace had been defeated by a novice.

The night of March 24/25 saw the last massive raid of the "Battle of Berlin;" 73 of the 811 bombers involved were lost and the Nachtjagd was credited with 82 *Abschüsse*. Five single-engine and 12 twin-engine NJ aircraft were lost.

During the month of March, the Luftwaffe command desperately tried to increase the effectiveness of night fighter operations. Elements of NJG 1 were regrouped in France. II./NJG 1 (the "feared" "Ghosts of St.-Trond") moved from Belgium to St.-Dizier, taking the place of II./NJG 4, who moved to Dijon. III./NJG 1 temporarily left the Netherlands (Twente) for Athies, also staying in France for two months. IV./NJG 1 took over from II./NJG 1 in St.-Trond. These movements were designed to counter Allied bombers flying over the north of France, a sector hitherto sparsely defended by night fighters. I./NJG 6 deployed to Illesheim; I./NJG 2 left the Netherlands for Kassel-Rothwesten; II./NJG 2 moved to Quackenbrück; III./NJG 2 moved to Langendiebach and Twente; II./NJG 3 moved to Langendiebach and Vechta; the Stab/NJG 5 moved to Athies, and III./NJG 5 to Brandis.

On the night of March 18/19, the young Günther Lomberg (left), pilot and adjutant with the Stab I./NJG 6, won the first of his three victories downing a Halifax. He is seen here with his radio operator, Uffz. Fritz Seith, on the muddy field at Gross Sachsenheim. Lomberg wore glasses, a physical defect that saw him rejected as a pilot at the beginning of the war. He survived the war.

# The Junkers Ju 88 G-1 and G-6

No longer "confined" to their "boxes", the *Zahme Sau* or *Verfolgungsnachtjagd* (pursuit interception night-hunting procedure) saw night fighters roaming over large areas of the Reich during RAF raids. With its bigger airframe, greater fuel capacity, longer endurance and more powerful armament, this in turn meant that the Junkers Ju 88 G-series became the standard Luftwaffe night fighter over the last two years of the war. The Ju 88 C-series—a barely disguised bomber that was only slightly faster than the RAF "heavies" it was hunting—had run out of steam during 1942. Toward the end of that year Junkers completed a mockup of a new, heavily revised version of the aircraft, the Ju 88 G. The Ju 88 V 58 (GI+BW) also known as the Ju 88 G V1, was the first test model to be trialed.

The G-series were the first Ju 88 variants not based on the Ju 88 bomber "A" fuselage. The G-1 had a redesigned nose, omitted the A-series' Bola ventral defensive gun position and featured a single "fisheye" armoured defensive weapon mount in the rear cockpit. It was fitted with the enlarged squared-off vertical fin/rudder tail unit and rear fuselage of the Ju 188 (making it slightly longer than the C-series) while the wing had extended and enlarged ailerons and the tailplanes featured extended tips. As with the C-series there was no standard armament fit, although the "G" usually toted a quartet of cannon in a ventral weapons pod.

Appearing during early 1944, the Ju 88 G-1 was powered by BMW 801 G-2 radial engines and carried a much larger and more modern radar suite—an additional FuG 350 Naxos or FuG 227 Flensburg homing device as well as the now-standard FuG 220 Lichtenstein SN-2 (90 MHz VHF) radar which the British knew little or nothing about until Mäckle landed in Suffolk in July 1944. Note the later SN-2d radar had the dipoles angled at 45° (frequency V). The G-6 versions were powered by Jumo 213A inline-V12 engines and often featured one or two 20-cm MG 151/20 cannon in a (*Schräge Musik*) slanting mount. Some of the final G-series models received new Jumo 213E engines and new radar installations, either the FuG 218 Neptun V/R or the latest FuG 240 Berlin N-1 cavity magnetron-based 30 GHz-band (centimetric) radar. However, the Jumo 213 E engines were always in short supply and only a small number of these were built. Production of the G-6 started during June 1944 and production peaked during November 1944 (some 300 built) while the total number constructed was around 1,280.

Compared to the Bf 110 G, the Ju 88 G was of course a much bigger airframe. All fuel could be carried internally and endurance was significantly greater than that of the Bf 110. One noticeable advantage of the larger airframe was the housing of the *Schrägbewaffnung* (slanting armament) in the rear fuselage; in the Bf 110—where fitted—it was enclosed with the crew. The roomier Ju 88 G cockpit meant that an additional crewmember could be carried and thus the radio/radar operator's workload could be shared. Although not a dedicated Mosquito "hunter," the G-6 could at least take on and/or evade Mosquito intruders. The Ju 88 G-1 was some 50 kph faster than the Bf 110 G-4 with external tanks. The G-series featured de-icing of the wing and tailplanes—the Ju 88 G-1 was equipped in many instances with two or three Kärcher-Heizgeräte. These were essentially petrol heaters, more colloquially known as Kärcher "ovens" and could be mounted in the rear fuselage or in each wing close to the wing leading edge between the engines and fuselage. A supply of air via the intakes located near the wing root was heated and then redistributed around the airframe for heating and de-icing.

Lt. Helmut Bunje flew both the Bf 110 and Ju 88 with NJG 6 and achieved victories in both types. Bunje achieved his first victory in his 4./NJG 6 Bf 110 G-4 over a Halifax on March 15, 1944. He was still flying with 4./NJG 6 when the Staffel converted to the Ju 88 G-1 in June 1944 and was then reequipped with the Ju 88 G-6 version in November 1944. In December 1944 Bunje returned his fifth kill, this time over a Lancaster. On February 23, 1945, he claimed three Lancasters and his final two kills were over Lancasters on 16 March 16, 1945, near Schwäbisch Hall, all in the Ju 88 G-6. Bunje noted that "in all important aspects the Ju 88—especially the Ju 88 G-6—was clearly superior to the Bf 110 G-4, particularly at altitude."

The RLM made its own decision on the comparable quality of the two types and decided, in the late summer of 1944, that Bf 110 production was to be curtailed, and in November 1944, the Bf 110 program was terminated. This was largely the result of continuing problems with the DB 605 E—planned to replace the DB 605 B in the Bf 110—and the superiority of the Ju 88.

Two views of the Ju 88 G-1 coded "4R+AK" of 2./NJG 2 in Quackenbrück. Note the single slanting weapon ahead of the windshield with muzzle-flash suppressor.

# The Normandy Campaign: June–August 1944

In the West Allied landings on the Continent were imminent and inevitable. On the German side, it was impossible to predict when or where. In the meantime, the Nachtjagd continued to counter the armadas of Bomber Command with varying degrees of success. In March 1944, over the following weeks, the Luftwaffe came up against a new Allied offensive aimed at transport networks. This so-called Transportation Plan was aimed at limiting the German military response to the invasion by crippling German rail networks and throwing German logistics into chaos.

On the night of March 26/27, while 705 bombers attacked Essen, a further 109 bombed the Belgian rail hub at Courtrai (Kortrijk). Ten victories were awarded to the Nachtjagd, while 12 four-engine bombers did not return to England. Following this German defensive failure—Bomber Command suffered losses of just 1 percent—on March 30/31 the RAF launched a "maximum effort" raid on Nuremberg, the "City of the NSDAP."

The night was clear and moonlit. The predicted protective high cloud cover failed to materialize, but the raid went ahead. Some 795 aircraft were dispatched—572 Lancasters, 214 Halifaxes and 9 Mosquitos. To quote from the official RCAF account: "a crystal-clear night greeted the airmen. To make matters worse, the normally invisible steam from the engine's exhaust condensed, creating clearly visible trails in the sky." The first night fighters appeared just before the bombers reached the Belgian border and the fierce battle that developed in the moonlight lasted for the next hour. Some 82 bombers were lost on the outward route and near the target. The carnage was reduced on the return flight, when most of the German fighters had to land, but 95 bombers were lost in all—64 Lancasters and 31 Halifaxes, 11.9 percent of the force dispatched. It was Bomber Command's biggest loss of the war and as one author put it, this was the Nachtjagd's "finest hour of the war." Altogether, 545 Commonwealth airmen died, more than RAF Fighter Command had lost during the Battle of Britain.

Dispatching such a force over such distances under very unfavorable conditions was probably an indication that Bomber Command felt that the Luftwaffe was already on the ropes. Nachtjagd losses were limited—five twin-engine and six single-engine aircraft and the *Experten* continued to score victories—but only 15 pilots achieved a first *Luftsieg* that night. If the night fighters had been able to repeat the feats of March 30/31, they could probably have done even greater damage to the British air offensive.

In March, some units moved temporarily. II./NJG 3 left Schleswig for Langendiebach and Vechta, the Stab/NJG 5 for Deelen and III./NJG 5 for Brandis.

Fifteen NJ pilots opened their score during the raid on Nuremberg on March 30/31. However, not all of them were fresh-faced novices. Hptm. Josef Krahforst, born in 1911 and a former naval aviator who served with 11./NJG 1 in 1943 before leading 2./NJG 4, scored 10 more victories before being shot down by a Mosquito intruder over Gelnhausen on the night of September 27/28, 1944.

On April 6, 1944, Fw. Rudolf Frank (3./NJG 3) was finally awarded the Ritterkreuz for the 42 victories he had won in such a short space of time. He was then promoted to Ofw. but his days were numbered. On the same day, Obstlt. Günther Radusch, Kommodore of NJG 2, was awarded the Eichenlaub for his 53 *Luftsiege*. On April 8, Ritterkreuze were awarded to Hptm. Leopold Fellerer, leading II./NJG 5, for his 34 victories (including two B-17s in January and five four-engine bombers on the night of January 20/21); and Ofw. Karl-Heinz Scherfling of 12./NJG 1 for his 29 *Abschüsse*. Scherfling was KIA on the night of July 20/21, another NJ ace shot down by a Mosquito.

The month of April saw a succession of attacks targeting mainly railway stations and tracks in Belgium and France. These included April 9/10: Villeneuve-St.-Georges and La Délivrance (Lille); April 10/11: Ghent, Tergniers, Tours, and Aulnoye. Among the successful Nachtjagd pilots was Hptm. Helmut Bergmann, Kapitän of 8./NJG 4, who downed eight

Lt. Georg Fengler of IV./NJG 1 (left) also scored his first victory in the raid on Nuremberg. He is seen here with his comrade and superior Schnaufer (right). Between them is Hptm. Hans-Joachim Jabs, recent Kommodore of NJG 1. Fengler scored as many as 15 victories, although at least six of these were unconfirmed. He was shot down by a Mosquito on March 21/22, 1945, and bailed out injured. After the war, Fengler joined the Schnaufer family winery and married Schnaufer's sister.

bombers in 46 minutes (19th–25th *Luftsiege*). On April 11, the Eichenlaub was awarded to Majors Rudolf Schoenert (Kdr of the single-engine NJGr 10) for his 61 *Abschüsse* and Wilhelm Herget (Kdr of I./NJG 4) for his 63. April 11/12: attack on the two major railway centers in Aachen with a "reduced force" of 250 bombers; April 18/19: Rouen, Juvisy.

On April 20, Oblt. Martin "Tino" Becker was awarded the Ritterkreuz for his 26 victories, including seven on the "famous" night of March 30/31. This former battlefield recce pilot, who had joined the Nachtjagd late in 1943, led 2./NJG 6. April 22/23: attack on Düsseldorf, with 47 victories awarded to the Nachtjagd. April 24/25: during a raid on Munich, Oblt. Schnaufer was credited with his 55th–57th victories. A larger force of some 637 bombers attacked Karlsruhe. Airborne from Venlo, Hptm. Modrow, Staka of 1./NJG 1, accounted for a 100 Sqn Lancaster and a 425 Sqn Halifax in his He 219 "G9+GK." April 26/27: Essen, Schweinfurt, and Villeneuve, with 28 bombers claimed by the Nachtjagd for 29 bombers lost—21 Lancasters from the Schweinfurt raid did not return, i.e., 9.3 percent. Schnaufer claimed another two of these and Bergmann three (his 26th–28th). Newly appointed Ritterkreuzträger Ofw. Rudolf Frank (3./NJG 3) claimed his 46th victim near Eindhoven but his Bf 110 G-4 was hit by debris and, although his comrades were able to bail out, he perished in his machine. He was posthumously awarded the Eichenlaub and the rank of Leutnant. Lt. Rolf Ebhardt of 8./NJG 1 downed a Lancaster over Troyes for his first *Abschuss*.

April 27/28: attacks on Friedrichshafen as well as the Belgian rail hub of Montzen and the French station of Aulnoye—47 *Luftsiege* were claimed by the Nachtjagd for the loss of 26 fighters. Oblt. Wilhelm Johnen, Staka of 6./NJG 5 airborne from Hagenau in his Bf 110, shot down a Lancaster near Strasbourg and a second Lancaster near the target. Intercepting a third bomber, his port engine was set alight by return fire, forcing him to make an emergency landing in Switzerland. To prevent Allied agents from studying the aircraft's sophisticated equipment, an agreement was reached between the German and Swiss governments. The Bf 110 was "scuttled" in exchange for the delivery of 12 Bf 109s to the Swiss Air Force. Johnen and his comrades were repatriated a few days later. Suspected for a time of having deliberately turned over his machine to the Swiss, the pilot was cleared, achieving 33 victories and earning the Ritterkreuz, awarded on October 29, 1944.

Ofw. Rudolf Frank poses on his Bf 110 G-4 with the Ritterkreuz he received on April 6. Three weeks later, he was killed and posthumously awarded the Eichenlaub.

With NJG 1 due to be redeployed in May, Kommodore Jabs flew to Belgium to check conditions at St.-Trond on the afternoon of April 29. The flight almost proved fatal. Returning to Deelen, he suddenly spotted four 132 Sqn Spitfire Mk IXs which turned in for an attack. After narrowly evading their opening salvos, Jabs saw that his only chance was to fly at his attackers. In two passes and bursts of gunfire, he knocked two of the Spitfires out of the unequal fight. Pursued by the two remaining enemy fighters, his own aircraft was riddled but he was able to put down at Deelen, scrambling clear of his Bf 110 before it was strafed and set on fire. These were Jabs's 44th and 45th victories—although slightly wounded, he had escaped lightly. At around this time, the Luftministerium put an end to day sorties, belatedly taking stock of the heavy losses suffered by the Nachtjagd in daylight hours.

The month of May saw an intensification of April's operations but, in addition to Franco-Belgian railway hubs—St.-Ghislain, Haine-St.-Pierre, Paris sector, Chambly, etc.—Bomber Command targeted airfields (Tours, Nantes, etc.), coastal batteries in the Pas-de-Calais, and troop concentrations (Mailly-le-Camp, Leopoldsburg, etc.). On the night of May 9/10, no fewer than 18 targets (Genneviliers, Annecy, etc.) were assigned to the bombers to force the enemy to break up its depleted forces. It would be tedious to list all the targets, as most of the fights that took place were skirmishes. With the guidance of the ground controllers, the Nachtjäger regularly shot down a handful of *Viermots*, but these were mere drops in the ocean. Despite the serious difficulties of the moment, some pilots continued to add to their score. On May 3/4 in the attack on Mailly, Hptm. Helmut Bergmann, Staka of 8./NJG 4, who was used to this type of series, downed five Lancasters (29th–33rd). On May 8/9, over Haine-St.-Pierre, the young Uffz. Konrad Beyer (1./NJG 4) shot down four bombers (3rd–6th).

In May, Bomber Command launched only three major attacks on the Reich: on May 21/22 over Duisburg with 532 bombers—28 *Luftsiege* were assigned to the Nachtjagd; on May 22/23 with 390 "heavies" over Dortmund and Braunschweig, the night fighters claimed 37 victories; on May 24/25, over the major rail hubs of Aachen, 32 *Abschüsse* were awarded.

In anticipation of the landings, aid to the resistance networks in occupied countries was stepped up. On the night of May 28/29, 23 "Carpetbaggers" loaded with material

On May 3/4, in the attack on Mailly-le-Camp, two Bf 110s from 3./NJG 4 were lost. Radio operator Julius Hahn was killed in one of them. He had been posted to Florennes with I./NJG 4 on January 2, 1944.

On May 9, Florennes airfield came under heavy attack from B-17s. The Ju 88 Gs of I./NJG 4 were moved to the spartan field strip at Cerfontaine.

for the Resistance were sent to the continent. Hptm. Josef Krahforst, Staka of 2./NJG 4, shot down one of them, a B-24 of the 801st BG that came down at Aaigem. The following night, May 29/30, Lt. Karl Kern (2./NJG 4), flying out of the field strip at Cerfontaine, intercepted another 801st BG B-24 that crashed at Sart-St.-Laurent for his first victory. Boiten's figures indicate that the Nachtjagd lost 41 aircraft and scored 267 victories during May 1944. As the fighting was limited and "accurate," it seems that 90 percent of these successes can be confirmed.

As disaster loomed for the Reich, a serious reshuffling took place within an increasingly depleted Nachtjagd. After two months on French soil, II./NJG 1 left St.-Dizier for St.-Trond, while III./NJG 1 left Athies for the Netherlands. They were replaced in Athies by the Stab/NJG 5 and III./NJG 5 from Deelen and Brandis respectively; in St.-Dizier by I./NJG 5 from Stendal. I./NJG 2 went to Langensalza and II./NJG 3 returned to Plantlünne. On May 8, II./NJG 4 left Dijon for Coulommiers; III./NJG 5 moved from Brandis to Athies; IV./NJG 5 left Brandis for Mainz-Finthen; II./NJG 101 left Manching for Parndorf and I./NJG 102 moved from Kitzingen to Powunden. II./NJG 5, based in Hagenau, was redesignated III./NJG 6 without any change to its command. A 4(Erg)./NJG 7 was created in Brieg—this was a redesignation of 12./KG 51, a unit equipped with Me 410s that had flown night fighter sorties over England. Most surprising of all was the transfer in early May of I./NJG 6 to Wiener-Neustadt and eight Bf 110s from II./NJG 6 to Ghedi in northern Italy. I. Gruppe operated in the Budapest sector, hunting RAF Wellingtons operating out of Italy to mine the Danube. However, it soon became apparent that Wiener-Neustadt was unsuitable for Nachtjäger and, from May 15, I./NJG 6 returned to Echterdingen before moving to Haifingen and then Kitzingen. On May 30, all of II./NJG 6 received orders to leave for Ghedi. On June 2, III./NJG 6 moved to Steinamanger (Hungary). With all these short-term movements, NJG 6 was barely an effective force.

On June 15, 1944, Lt. Karl Kern's 2./NJG 4 crew received the EK II for their victory on May 29/30 over a 801st BG B-24 "Carpetbagger." It was their only success, however, as they were shot down soon afterward. The pilot was the only survivor.

## Nachtjagd Unit Deployments, June 1, 1944

| | | | |
|---|---|---|---|
| Stab/NJG 1 | Bönninghardt | I./NJG 6 | Kitzingen |
| I./NJG 1 | Venlo | II./NJG 6 | Ghedi |
| II./NJG 1 | St.-Dizier | III./NJG 6 | Hagenau |
| III./NJG 1 | Twente/Leeuwaarden | IV./NJG 6 | Otopeni/Zilistea |
| IV./NJG 1 | St.-Trond | I./NJG 7 | Münster-Handorf |
| Schulstaffel NJG 1 | Twente | 4.(Erg.)/NJG 7 | Brieg |
| Stab NJG 2 | Deelen | Stab I./NJG 100 | Biala-Podlaska |
| I./NJG 2 | Langensalza | 1./NJG 100 | Biala-Podlaska |
| II./NJG 2 | Quackenbrück | 2./NJG 100 | Focsani/Otopeni |
| III./NJG 2 | Langendiebach/Twente | 3./NJG 100 | Radom |
| Stab/NJG 3 | Stade | Stab II./NJG 100 | Nisch |
| I./NJG 3 | Vechta | 4./NJG 100 | Reval-Laksberg |
| II./NJG 3 | Plantlünne | 5./NJG 100 | Gross Beckereck |
| III./NJG 3 | Stade | 6./NJG 100 | Krumowo |
| IV./NJG 3 | Westerland | Stab/NG 101 | Ingolstadt |
| Stab/NJG 4 | Chenay | I./NJG 101 | Ingolstadt |
| I./NJG 4 | Florennes | II./NJG 101 | Parndorf |
| II./NJG 4 | Coulommiers | Stab NJG 102 | Kitzingen |
| III./NJG 4 | Juvincourt | I./NJG 102 | Powunden |
| Stab/NJG 5 | Athies | II./NJG 102 | Echterdingen |
| I./NJG 5 | St.-Dizier | 1./NJG 200 | Gross Beckereck |
| III./NJG 5 | Athies | 4./NJG 200 | Neuburg |
| IV./NJG 5 | Mainz-Finthen | 5./NJG 200 | Focsani |
| Stab/NJG 6 | Schleissheim | I./NJGr 10 | Werneuchen, Finow, Westerwald |

On the night of June 2/3, Bomber Command attacked positions in the Pas-de-Calais, while 18 *Abschüsse* (16 certain) were scored by NJGs 1, 4, and 5, with almost all the bombers falling in France. The die was cast. And indeed, in the early hours of June 6, 1944, the Normandy landings began.

To be closer to the new front, II./NJG 2 left Butzweilerhof for Coulommiers to operate with II./NJG 4. The fighting over France was a series of skirmishes with bombers engaged in small formations on various targets: troop concentrations, roads and railways leading to the Normandy front, fuel depots, etc. The fighting exhausted the outnumbered Nachtjäger, which were subjected to bombing raids over their airfields as well as Mosquito attacks over the Allied bridgeheads. In addition, fuel was in short supply due to the disorganization of transport. On top of all that, German antiaircraft defenses shot down several Nachtjäger.

On June 6/7, 13 victories were awarded to NJGs 2, 4, and 5; on June 7/8, 37 *Abschüsse* were won over France; on June 9, Hptm. Helmut Bergmann, Staka of 8./NJG 4, was awarded the Ritterkreuz for his 34 victories; on June 9/10, six bombers crashed in France but the Nachtjagd lost three aircraft; on June 10/11, 20 bombers were shot down, with Hptm. Paul Zorner (Stab III./NJG 5) adding four more to his record (49th–51st), as did Lt. Walter Briegleb of 10./NJG 3 (5th–8th); on June 11/12, the Nachtjagd won no victories but lost three aircraft, all probable Mosquito victims, Hptm. Fritz Söthe (4./NJG 4), an ace with 14 victories, was wounded.

On June 12/13, the main targets were the railway installations at Cambrai and Amiens. For once, the Nachtjagd was correctly directed and 33 four-engine aircraft were lost. Ofw. Reinhard Kollak (8./NJG 4) was credited with three victories (20th–22nd), while Hptm. Heinz-Wolfgang Schnaufer (IV./NJG 1), Hptm. Ernst-Wilhelm Modrow of 1./NJG 1 (20th–22nd), and Maj. Wilhelm Herget (Stab I./NJG 4) downed two bombers (71st–72nd); on the night of June 14/15, of the 786 bombers engaged over France, only five fell victim to the Nachtjagd; on the night of June 15/16, 10 bombers were shot down in the north (Douai, Lille, Béthune, etc.). Obstlt. Helmut Lent, Kommodore of NJG 1, claimed three *Abschüsse*, reaching 100 victories.

While the Nachtjagd was decimated by the relentless fighting, Bomber Command also had to take a breather. By mid-June, the main targets were still the communication routes in France, but V1 sites had to be added—the British population was now terrorized by the indiscriminate firing of these missiles—as well as synthetic fuel factories in Germany. Confident of having weakened the enemy in France, Bomber Command devoted itself to the Reich and the V1 sites. On June 22/23, they returned to the railway centers in France (Reims, Laon, etc.). Ten bombers were shot down by the fighters at St Quentin, Amiens, Cambrai, etc.; on June 24/25, hoping (in vain) to get rid of the V1s raining down on London, 740 bombers pounded the

Hptm. Helmut Bergmann (8./NJG 4), known for his victory "series," received the Ritterkreuz on June 9, 1944.

Victory confirmation for June 25, 1944, awarded to Oblt. Rolf Klages, Staka of 3./NJG 4 on downing a Lancaster that fell near Abbeville during an attack on a V1 site. It is stated that this was in collaboration with a Flak battery. A former FAGr.2 reconnaissance pilot, Klages was wounded on July 5 when he shot down his second victim; he apparently never flew again.

launch sites in the Pas-de-Calais. Taking advantage of this concentration, NJGs 2, 3, 4, and 5 shot down no fewer than 37 of them, with several aces (Lent, Semrau, Rökker, etc.) adding to their scoreboards.

On June 28/29, Bomber Command attacked rail infrastructure as far east as Metz to disrupt links with the Normandy front, with 21 bombers lost. On the night of June 30/July 1, the railway at Vierzon was attacked—the Nachtjagd reacted vigorously with 16 victories. Obstlt. Günther Radusch (NJG 2) won two *Luftsiege* (63rd and 64th), Hptm. Paul Zorner (I./NJG 5) his 55th. On July 4/5, another large-scale Bomber Command assault took place on railway hubs and V1 sites—48 bombers fell in France, with some victories going to aces like Walter Borchers, Fritz Söthe (back in action) and Hermann Greiner. On July 7/8, the Ninth Air Force launched a major attack on V1 sites, committing 35 B-26 Marauders in support. 51 RAF four-engine aircraft were reported to have fallen victim to the Tagjagd, as well as 10 B-26s.

On July 12/13, the RAF carried out another operation on rail infrastructure and V1 sites, losing nine bombers. On July 14/15, in addition to V1 sites, the bombers targeted Villeneuve-St.-Georges and Revigny. Seven four-engine bombers were lost, two

Hptm. Werner Hoffmann scored his 33rd *Abschuss* over a Lancaster near Dieppe on June 27/28. He survived the war with 52 *Abschüsse* to his credit.

On the night of July 7/8, Lt. Erich Jung (6./NJG 2) shot down two four-engine aircraft (his 9th and 10th) near Creil before his Ju 88 G-1 was hit by a night fighter. He is seen here in the early hours of the morning, still in his flight suit, on the platform at Creil station on his way back to Coulommiers with his crew (from left: gunner Hans Reinagel, Jung, and radio operator Walter Heidenreich).

being credited to a future Ritterkreuzträger, Oblt. Ernst-Georg Drünkler (1./NJG 5). During the night of July 18/19, Bomber Command attacked rail installations in force, losing 35 bombers, two of which were shot down by Obstlt. Lent near Reims (105th and 106th). On the night of July 26/27, in appalling weather, the bombers set off for the marshaling yard at Givors. A clever young crew from 2./NJG 2 deduced the route of some four-engine bombers on the basis of the Window drops. Lt. Otto Huchler shot down a Lancaster north of Vannes and then a second. But these were his first and last victories, as a machine-gunner from 619 Sqn, his last victim, fired a burst that killed Huchler outright. Although wounded, his two comrades were able to jump.

Outnumbered and hampered by a lack of fuel and technical assistance, the Nachtjagd aircraft could hardly operate, even if their crews tried the impossible. As well as flying into a desperate military situation, they were forced to carry out ground-strafing missions (*Nachtschlachteinsätze*) for which the crews were not trained. Losses were severe, as the twin-engine planes had to fly at very low altitudes. For example, III./NJG 5, ordered to strafe Allied bridgeheads (Operation *Heidelberg*), lost half a dozen aircraft on the night of August 3/4. Among those lost was the Staka of 9./NJG 5, Oblt. Gerhard Wagner, holder of 13 victories (he was captured). Hptm. Autenrieth strafed troops landed in the Bay of Mont-St.-Michel with his 6./NJG 4.

On the night of August 6/7, 8./NJG 4 lost two Bf 110 G-4s with their crews in the Mortain/Avranches sector. One of the pilots was the renowned Hptm. Helmut Bergmann, Staka and Ritterkreuzträger with 36 *Luftsiege*. This "series" specialist (six victories on April 10/11, 1944, three on April 26/27, and six on May 3/4) fell victim to either a Mosquito night fighter or ground fire. His Bf 110 crashed on a road leading to the front, temporarily blocking

The hell over Normandy cut short several meteoric NJ careers. The young crew of Ofhr. Johannes Naskrent (2./NJG 2) arrived at Coulommiers and shot down two four-engine aircraft near Amiens on the night of June 12/13. On June 14, Naskrent and his crew were themselves shot down by a P-38 near Etampes (an incident not included in the loss lists) but escaped without harm. On August 7/8, Naskrent brought down two more Lancasters near Fécamp, but shortly afterward his Ju 88 G-1 was hit by a Mosquito near Coulommiers, with only the gunner surviving. A poor-quality but rare snapshot taken at Châteaudun during the presentation of the EK II.

the advance of a Panzer column. On the night of August 7/8, Bomber Command carried out a major operation to the south of Caen during the fight for the town. Ten victories were won over Le Havre, Lisieux, Yvetot, Fécamp, etc., three of which were credited to Hptm. Heinz Rökker (Staka of 2./NJG 2 and African veteran) who achieved 40 *Abschüsse*. On August 9, faced with the Allied advance, I./NJG 2 moved from Châteaudun to Dijon.

With the Wehrmacht falling back, Bomber Command was able to step up its attacks on the Reich. On August 21, near Juvincourt, an aircraft from 7./NJG 4 was damaged in a transfer flight. Around this time that III./NJG 4 evacuated this airfield, which it had occupied for two years. Other Nachtjagd units followed: I./NJG 2 went to Kassel-Rothwesten, II./NJG 2 returned to Butzweilerhof, II./NJG 4 left Coulommiers for Rhein-Main, I./NJG 5 departed St.-Dizier for East Prussia, while III./NJG 5 abandoned Athies.

The Normandy Campaign was catastrophic for the Luftwaffe. However, it is difficult to give a precise figure for Nachtjagd losses, as the lists are incomplete. If we disregard the *Fernnachtjagd* (I./NJG 2) in 1940/41, for the first time the night fighter arm, a defensive weapon, was used offensively in the dangerous task of ground strafing, so-called *Nachtschlachteinsätze*. A lack of aircraft meant that the Luftwaffe had to divert night fighters with their sophisticated equipment and trained crews from the task for which they had been designed.

Coulommiers, home to II./NJG 2 and II./NJG 4, was heavily bombed during the battle of Normandy. The Americans discovered many wrecks on the airfield.

## Assaults on the Reich

At the start of the invasion the Bf 110s of Stab and I./NJG 3 left Stade and Vechta to establish themselves at Le Culot. IV./NJG 3 also moved to Melsbroek in Belgium. In this way, the two Gruppen could fight over France as well as against the bombers flying toward Germany. Le Culot did not seem particularly suitable for night fighters. But necessity dictated.

On June 9, four Ritterkreuze were awarded: to Hptm. Paul Zorner, Kommander of II./NJG 5, for his 48 successes; to Oblt. Hans-Heinz Augenstein, Staka of 12./NJG 1 (42 v.); to Hptm. Helmut Bergman, Staka 8./NJG 4 (34 v.), and to Hptm. Ludwig Meister, recovering Staka from 1./NJG 4 (38 v.).

A real danger now threatened the Nachtjäger, and not just the "greenhorns:" the Mosquitos engaged in *Flower* operations hunted down any twin-engine aircraft they encountered. On the night of June 14/15, I./NJG 4 operating over Cambrai claimed two victories. On the return to Charleroi, F/Lt. Arthur Burbridge, a pilot with 85 Sqn, intercepted and shot down a "Ju 188," in fact a Ju 88 G-1 flown by the great ace and Kommandeur of I./NJG 4, Maj. Wilhelm Herget. The Junkers crashed at Pont-à-Celles. Although Herget, unlike his two injured crew, was unhurt, he was briefly rested. The following night, June 15/16, two Bf 110 G-4s fell victim to Mosquito attacks near Tongeren and Beauvechain (two killed). These often-fatal attacks handicapped the German defense.

Maj. Wilhelm Herget decorating his I./NJG 4 airmen at Florennes. The ace was shot down by a Mosquito on the night of June 14/15.

Bomber Command's first raid of the month on the Reich took place on the night of June 16/17 against the Sterkrade synthetic fuel factory. Of the 321 bombers involved, 31 were lost (almost 10 percent)—37 victories were awarded to the NJ. Drewes, Schnaufer, and Briegleb all took part. Seven NJ twins were lost. On June 21/22, two raids were launched against hydrogenation plants at Wesseling and Scholven with 246 bombers. Some 56 victories were confirmed—in fact 10 more than the RAF's actual losses (i.e. more than 10 percent). Two night fighters were lost. This was nonetheless—in percentage terms—one of Bomber Command's worse loss rates of the war. More than 160 night fighters had been launched including the He 219s of I./NJG 1 who enjoyed one of their "best" nights of the war, with 14 kills shared among the five crews, including four for Hauptleute Modrow and Strüning

On June 24, four aces were decorated: Hptm. Heinz-Wolfgang Schnaufer, Kommandeur of IV./NJG 1, received the Eichenlaub for his 84 victories; Hptm. Gerhard Raht, Staka of 4./NJG 3, was awarded the RK for 34 *Abschüsse*; Oblt. Erich Weißflog, Hans-Joachim Jabs's loyal radio man, was also awarded the Ritterkreuz, having taken part in 48 victories. He had been attached to the Stab/NJG 1 since March 1944; and Ofw. Kurt Bundrock, also with Stab/NJG 1, Funker to Knacke (until his death) before flying with Streib. He took part in 49 *Luftsiege*.

Highly committed to its attacks on railways and V1 sites, on June 18/19 the RAF set out again for Wesseling and Scholven with 364 aircraft, of which only five failed to return. None of these aircraft was claimed by the Nachtjagd, as they had been misdirected. On June 26, a III./NJG 102 was set up in Kitzingen with contributions from the FFS B19. On the night of July 12/13, Ju 88 G-1 coded "4R+UR" (WNr. 712273) of 7./NJG 2 and based at Volkel, landed at RAF Woodbridge in the east of England. Undoubtedly one of the most

Mäckle's Ju 88 G-1 coded "4R+UR" seen under guard in Woodbridge, England. Note the FuG 227 Flensburg radar homing antennas (azimuth aerials) mounted on both wing leading edges. The elevation aerials were located above and below the starboard wing outboard—this equipment became redundant overnight when RAF specialists realized that it homed onto their Monica tail-warning radar emissions. Note the air intake at the port wing root supplying the onboard "ovens" for airframe de-icing, an innovation on the G-series of Ju 88 night fighters.

important German aircraft to fall into Allied hands, it was equipped with the (unjammable thus far by the British) FuG 220 Lichtenstein SN-2 and the unknown FuG 227 Flensburg radar homer. It was being flown on a North Sea patrol by Uffz. Hans Mäckle in the early hours of July 13. According to his own postwar account Mäckle had taken off from Twente and after nearly five hours was running low on fuel and unable to break out of thick cloud cover or raise base. He had instructed his crew to prepare to bail out when his flight engineer informed the pilot that he had no parachute. Miraculously breaking out of the cloud at 200 meters, they found themselves over an airfield and landed. Mäckle had made the error of flying a reciprocal compass course. His aircraft would reveal many of the Luftwaffe's secrets.

The crew of Ofw. Karl-Heinz Scherfling. From left: Fw. Herbert Winkler (gunner), Ofw. Scherfling, and Fw. Herbert Scholz (radio). Only the latter survived the loss of their aircraft at Mol.

Ceremony in honor of Ritterkreuzträger Ofw. Karl-Heinz Scherfling. His wife, a Luftwaffe auxiliary, says her last farewell.

Bomber Command returned to the Reich on July 20/21 with 158 aircraft that raided a synthetic fuel plant at Homberg (20 Lancasters lost) and 166 bombers (eight lost) over Bottrop. The Nachtjagd lost two *Experte* pilots: the Bf 110 G-4 of Ofw. Karl-Heinz Scherfling (12./NJG 1) fell victim to a 169 Sqn Mosquito near Mol. Scherfling had 33 victories and the RK since April 1944. Only the wounded machine-gunner was able to bail out; Hptm. Martin Drewes, Kommandeur of III./NJG 1, shot down two *Viermots* in the Bottrop raid (his 43rd and 44th) but the explosion of the second near Haarle destroyed his Bf 110 G-4, forcing the wounded crew to evacuate.

On July 23/24, the RAF attacked Kiel and its major shipyards. Only three of the 620 bombers engaged were claimed by an increasingly overwhelmed Nachtjagd. To surprise the Nachtjagd, Bomber Command switched from north to south, launching 614 aircraft at Stuttgart on July 24/25. Some 25 bombers did not return, with around 15 attributed to the Nachtjäger. On July 25/26, 550 four-engine bombers returned to Stuttgart, their favorite target. Fifteen were lost, with around 10 going to the Nachtjagd, which lost around 11 twins. Following the attacks on Stuttgart, II./NJG 1 left Deelen for Echterdingen in southern Germany.

Fw. Stein with the cushion bearing Scherfling's decorations.

Hptm. Martin Drewes (III./NJG 1) was wounded in action over the Netherlands, caught by the explosion of his 44th victim on the night of July 20/21, 1944.

## Ritterkreuze Awards

On July 27, no fewer than 10 Ritterkreuze were awarded:

- Oblt. Heinz Rökker, Staka of 2./NJG 2 and veteran of the African battles, for 35 victories (in fact 40 at the time of the award);
- Hptm. Martin Drewes (III./NJG 1), wounded on July 20/21, for 44 victories;
- Oblt. Hermann Greiner, Staka of 11./NJG 1, 54 v. (four B-17s by day);
- Oblt. Werner Baake, Staka 2./NJG 1, for 33 kills;
- Ofw. Wilhelm Gänsler, gunner for Ludwig Becker and later for Schnaufer, who took part in 115 successes with his pilots;
- Hptm. Heinz-Martin Hadeball, Kommandeur of I./NJG 6, recently transferred to 3./NJG 10, for his 32 victories;
- Ofw. Erich Handke, radio operator to several NJG 1 aces, for his 59 "participations" (including three during the day);
- Kommandeur Herget's loyal radio operator (I./NJG 4), Ofw. Hans Liebherr (wounded on June 14/15), who took part in 68 actions (11 during the day);
- Hptm. Friedrich-Karl "Nasen" Müller, ex-JG 300 and Staka of 1.NJGr 10, for 33 kills;
- Oblt. Dietrich Schmidt, Staka of 8./NJG 1, for 32 kills (including a Mosquito).

On July 27, Oblt. Werner Baake (2./NJG 1) received the Ritterkreuz. On January 27/28, 1944, his Bf 110 G-4 was hit by the debris of his 24th victim and, although he was able to bail out, his radio operator was killed.

The Nachtjagd had a serious set-to with Bomber Command on the night of August 12/13 when 379 bombers flew to Braunschweig and 297 to Rüsselsheim—47 were shot down, 49 claimed. Eight victories were credited to "greenhorns" as their first victory and, once again, the *Experten* came out on top.

On August 16/17, distant Stettin was targeted by 348 bombers, which lost five of their own. At the same time, 348 four-engine bombers attacked Kiel, with the loss of five aircraft. The NJ issued 10 claims. Six twin-engine aircraft were shot down (one by Flak, one by a Mosquito). On August 18/19, the results were worse—289 bombers attacked Bremen and 234 returned to the Sterkrade factory. Only five aircraft were shot down and two *Luftsiege* credited. On August 19, Hptm. Ernst Modrow, ex-Lufthansa pilot and Staka of 1./NJG 1, was awarded the Ritterkreuz for his 27 victories (including a Mosquito).

During his short stay in Le Culot in June/July 1944, Obstlt. Helmut Lent visited his IV./NJG 1 comrades at St.-Trond. He is seen here on the terrace of Schloss Mielen with Hptm. Schnaufer (awarded the Schwerter on July 30 for 89 victories) and Maj. Jabs. Lent was the first Nachtjäger to receive the Diamonds.

Two views of a I./NJG 6 Bf 110 G-4 photographed during the summer of 1944. Note the flame suppressors on the nose-mounted cannon. One of the two slanting cannons is visible in the rear cockpit (top).

On August 25/26, 412 Lancasters bombed Rüsselsheim, with a further 200 taking on Darmstadt. With France almost completely liberated, those remaining detection centers in France could no longer provide accurate information on the bombers' track. Despite this major handicap, 23 aircraft did not return to England, while 26 night fighters were awarded victories. It should be noted that 10 or so of the victorious pilots had between one and four victories, i.e. aces in the making. On the night of August 26/27, Bomber Command launched another double attack: 372 Lancasters hit Kiel and 174 Königsberg. Twenty-seven were lost (including five on "gardening" sorties). Sixteen victories were awarded (including the first for an NJ "greenhorn"). It is not known how many twin-engine fighters were lost but, at Stade, a Mosquito shot down the Ju 88 G-1 flown by Lt. Achim Woeste, Staka of 7./NJG 3 and an ace with 10 victories. The crew was killed.

Despite its losses, the lack of aircraft and fuel and its numerical inferiority, the Nachtjagd showed that it still had some bite on the night of August 29/30 when Bomber Command attacked Stettin with 405 aircraft and Königsberg with 189. Thirty-nine four-engine aircraft were lost (50 claimed) as well as seven Ju 88/Bf 110s. Faced with the Allied advance, the NJ units still in Belgium evacuated to Germany late August/early September (Florennes was evacuated around September 4).

## The Heinkel He 219 –"A Missed Opportunity" Part 2

On July 1, 1943, Hptm. Hans-Dieter Frank had taken over the reins at I./NJG 1 and claimed seven RAF bombers between July 25/26 and September 5/6 at the controls of an He 219. He was killed on the night of September 27/28 when his He 219 was involved in a midair collision with an Me 110 G-4 from the Geschwaderstab NJG 1. Earlier that month, on the night of September 5/6, Ritterkreuz winner Oblt. Heinz Strüning, Staffelkapitän of 3./NJG 1, was hit by the return fire of an intended victim and was forced to bail out of "G9+GL" (WNr. 190010). His BF Willi Bleier was killed. In January 1944 Kommandeur I./NJG 1 Manfred Meurer was killed at the controls of an He 219—the second CO to lose his life in the machine. There were still many problems affecting He 219 serviceability—in fact I./NJG 1 still had only three serviceable machines on strength as late as December 1943. Serviceability does not seem to have improved greatly during 1944. Developed under the pressure of events, shortcuts and omissions were to be expected. Of course, the type's continuing difficulties were political as well. Messerschmitt and Junkers were firms in which the Reich held most shares, i.e. virtually state-owned companies. Added to this were the internal ties between the RLM and Junkers, which once again surfaced here—Junkers were resolutely supported by the Generalluftzeugmeister Milch and continued to push hard to have Heinkel's night fighter replaced with their multirole Ju 388.

Oberst Dietrich Peltz was one of the members of the Generalstab der Luftwaffe responsible for deciding the fate of the He 219. He had previously asked Herrmann of *Wilde Sau* fame to evaluate the Heinkel night fighter. In an annex to his report, Herrmann stated categorically that single-engine day fighters deployed at night could just as easily intercept the Mosquito as they had the performance necessary to intercept the cursed wooden RAF twin. No advocate of the costly Heinkel, Milch was enthusiastic "but for the Inspector of Night Fighters, it was a bitter pill to swallow," Herrmann wrote. After all, it was Kammhuber who had to sign the order creating the Nachtjagdversuchskommando (NJVK or Experimental Night Fighter Command) at Brandenburg-Briest. The single-engine night fighters enjoyed several months of successes, but the onset of poor winter weather took a toll of men and machines.

Heinkel continued to insist that the He 219 was the only dedicated Mosquito-hunter (*Moskito-Jagd*) in the Luftwaffe's inventory and to stress that it was some 30 kph faster—on the same engines—than the Ju 388. The He 219 *could* catch a Mosquito at full throttle—but usually required the advantage of height. The first Mosquito shot down by an He 219 was no earlier than May 6/7, 1944—Oblt. Werner Baake, StaKa of 2./NJG 1 downed an LNSF Mosquito returning from Leverkusen at 8,000 meters over the Netherlands. Later StaKa of 3./NJG 1, Oblt. Josef Nabrich claimed an LNSF Mosquito heading for the German capital on the night of June 10/11, 1944, his first Mosquito and his sixth claim at the controls of an He 219. He claimed a second Mosquito the following night, chasing his prey for nearly 400 kilometers before shooting it down near Salzwedel, 160 kilometers north of Berlin.

In terms of combat operations June 1944 was the most "successful" month for the He 219—37 enemy aircraft destroyed, including five Mosquitos. Set against this was the loss of nine I./NJG 1 He 219s in accidents, following the loss of 10 machines during the previous month. Only 15 new-build Heinkel He 219s were delivered during May 1944. June 1944 also saw the establishment of an He 219 training Staffel—Schulstaffel NJG 1. This was short-lived and by late August its He 219s had gone.

Elsewhere Kammhuber's demand for series production of 1,200 He 219s and his insistence that the future of the Nachtjagd depended on it were steps too far for the RLM. By the summer of 1944 an embittered Kammhuber had been (re)moved to Norway and had given up the fight for the He 219. The opportunity for the He 219 to make a difference had passed. Former Junkers employee Heinz Nowarra writing in the April 1962 issue of *Jägerblatt* insisted that there had been no competitor type with similar performance available: "the Ju 88 G-1 was not it, nor was the Ju 88 G-6 with the better Jumo 213. And even if it was now called the Ju 188 or Ju 388, it was still a Ju 88." Critical of the RLM's refusal to order series production of the He 219, his assessment that this "sealed the defeat of the Nachtjagd" is an exaggeration.

In the end the He 219 never went into large-scale production—it was a complex machine demanding many tens of thousands of man-hours to build and construction never *averaged* much more than 13 machines per month (25 examples left the factory in both April and September 1944). Only around 195 machines reached operational units, the majority of these from the early summer of 1944. Even though the He 219 found its way onto the Sauer's *Jäger-Not* (emergency fighter) program, there were too many in the Luftwaffe hierarchy of the opinion that the He 219 carried few advantages over existing types. Production was wholly insufficient to decisively impact the outcome of the bombing war. Was it as good as its "reputation"? In a post-war assessment Eric "Winkle" Brown found the He 219 to be "underpowered," making single-engine flight tricky. Better performance was hampered by the lack of availability of new uprated engines. Had it been more effective against Mosquitos, it may well have had a better claim.

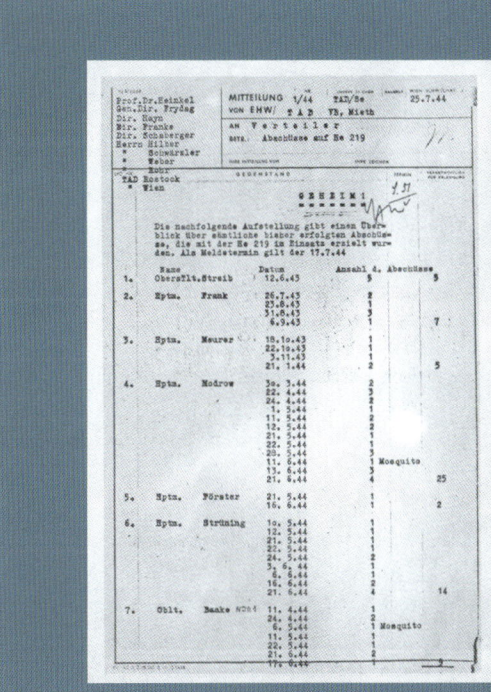

Page 1 of an internal Heinkel document dated July 25, 1944, listing all victories achieved by the He 219—the type had made its combat debut over a year earlier. (via Permann)

In total some 150 Allied machines were claimed shot down by He 219 pilots but over 100 He 219s were lost out of a production run of some 330 machines. The ejection seats were used on as many as 25 occasions. The first crew to save their lives with the ejection seats, then called *Katapult Anlage*, lit. catapult apparatus, was Uffz. Perbix and his Bordfunker on the night of April 10/11, 1944.

Venlo, summer 1944. Oblt. Josef Nabrich of 3./NJG 1 (center) poses for with his regular BF, Fw. Fritz Habicht (left). Nabrich filed some 12 claims at the controls of a He 219, his last on the night of August 12/13, 1944. He was killed during a strafing attack on Münster-Handorf on November 27, 1944.

## In Profile:
# Heinkel He 219 A-0 "G9+FK," 2./NJG 1

Heinkel He 219 A-0 coded "G9+FK" of 2./NJG 1 flown by Hptm. Ernst-Wilhelm Modrow, Venlo, April 1944. Radar equipment was the FuG 220 Lichtenstein SN-2 and the FuG 202 in the central nose position for both long- and short-range interception capability respectively.

# In the East: January–September 1944

January saw the creation in the Baltic States of the Ju 88-equipped 4./NJG 100 based at Reval-Laksberg (now Tallinn in Estonia). Lt. Klaus Scheer of this Staffel had his finest hour on the night of March 6/7, 1944 when he downed five Soviet PS-84s in the Narva area (Estonia) at the controls of his Ju 88 C-6 coded "W7+BM" before landing back at Reval. He accounted for four DB3-Fs on the night of March 9/10 during a raid by over 500 Soviet bombers on the Estonian capital of Tallinn, all later confirmed by Luftflotte 1. He ended the war with 24 night victories. That same night his comrade Uffz. Otto Holler achieved four *Abschüsse* in a row during the raid on Tallinn, achieving ace status. He was shot down and killed by return fire from his last victim—his kills were all later confirmed by Luftflotte 6. Hptm. Theodor Bellinghausen (4./NJG 100) also achieved ace status during the Tallinn raid, while Ofw. Karl Strohecker of 3./NJG 100 claimed a DB-6 and a "Martin" SB-2 for his fourth and fifth *Luftsiege*.

On February 12, 1944, according to an organization chart showing the strength of the night fighter units in Romania, IV./NJG 6 had 20 Bf 110s in flying order, 2./NJG 100 eight Ju 88s, and 10./JG 301 six Bf 109s. Up to the end of March 1944, the Nachtjagd detachments in Romania suffered minor losses, often due to the difficulties of maintaining the aircraft on the poor runways. This relative calm was not to last, however.

On March 9, 1944, a Ju 88 C-6 of the "new" 4./NJG 100 was shot down in combat at Järva-Jaani in Estonia. Pilot Uffz. Otto Holler was killed along with his two crew. The death card describes him as an ace.

# In Profile:
## Major Alois Lechner

Lechner remains another little-known night fighter ace in the USSR. Born in Bavaria in 1911, before the war he was a Flugkapitän with Lufthansa and therefore skilled on instruments. Flying in a transport unit at the start of the war, he later served as an instructor at an instrument training school (Blindflugschule). In late 1941, he joined 9./NJG 2, returned several victories and then took command of 10./NJG 5, which was temporarily deployed in the East. He remained on this front, moving to 1./NJG 100, and began to score regularly. On the night of October 27/28, 1943, as Staffelkapitän of 1./NJG 100 flying from Stary-bychow and guided by night-fighting train *Sumatra I*, he claimed no fewer than seven Soviet bombers downed—four of these were IL-4s bombing the rail junction at Minsk. On January 1, 1944, he took command of I./NJG 100, succeeding Hptm. Rudolf Schoenert who had returned his two final Eastern Front *Abschüsse* on the night of October 27/28. Lechner was awarded the Ritterkreuz on February 5, 1944 after 42 victories. He won three more up until February 23, when his Ju 88 C coded "V4+MT" was hit by ground fire. Seriously wounded, Lechner crashed his aircraft on Brigade Leonow airfield and was later reported MIA with his crew. Only his radio operator returned from Soviet captivity after the war. Lechner achieved 26 *Abschüsse* with the aid of the radar train *Sumatra I* from July 1943 to the time of his death in February 1944.

A poor-quality but rare view of Hptm. Alois Lechner (right) and his crew about to depart on a night sortie in the East. Note the 16-dipole *Matratze* antenna array of the FuG 202 in the nose of his Ju 88 C-6.

## In the East: January–September 1944

### In Profile:
## Bf 110 F coded "2Z+AF", IV./NJG 6

Lütje's Bf 110 displays the double chevrons of command and the yellow rear fuselage Eastern Front theater band and has a light blue-gray night fighter finish. Starboard lower wing surfaces were probably black, an ID feature.

While the Nachtjagd was wearing itself out in a desperate fight over Normandy and the Reich, night fighters were operating on other fronts. II./NJG 6 had been sent to Ghedi to operate in northern Italy. It soon became apparent that the lack of ground guidance was hampering efforts. Although one or two Wellingtons were claimed, losses occurred quickly, including that of Ofw. Helmut Treynogga (6./NJG 6), who was interned in Switzerland on March 15. Once again disoriented, he was killed near Perugia. On June 12, II./NJG 6 reached Echterdingen and then Venlo.

III./NJG 6 based at Steinamanger (Hungary) operated against Soviet aircraft as well as USAAF and RAF aircraft from Italy. On the night of June 11/12, a Mitchell was shot down in the Zagreb sector. On the night of June 26/27, five Wellingtons were claimed over Hungary. On July 6/7, no fewer than 14 Wellingtons were awarded near Fels-am-Wagram. Among the victors was Oblt. Johnen returned from his Swiss internment. III. Gruppe was to receive Ju 88s but deliveries were canceled, probably in view of the losses in the West, and retained Bf 110s until October. IV./NJG 6 at Bucharest-Otopeni and the handful of single-engine aircraft from 10./JG 301 were supported by the Ju 88s of 2./NJG 100 at Focsani. On April 29, 6./JG 301 (equipped with Bf 109s) moved into Targsorul Nou. However, its pilots were as inexperienced as those of 10./JG 301.

## Romanian Oilfields

IV./NJG 6 was established in mid-1943 to defend the Ploesti oilfields (Romania) under Kommandeur Lütje who had been awarded the RK on June 1, 1943. His most notable exploit was the downing of three Lancaster and three Halifax bombers (his victories 23–28) on the night of March 13/14, 1943. The first *Alarmstart* (scramble) received by the new IV./NJG 6 occurred on August 1, 1943—a daylight sortie to counter the famous American *Tidal Wave* mission targeting Ploesti. The Allied bombing campaign against the Romanian oilfields grew in intensity during the spring of 1944. By day it was led by the huge forces available to the USAAF Fifteenth Air Force. By night, the RAF's 205 Group based in Italy around Foggia flew against Romanian oilfields and industrial targets—the only British air group in World War II to operate under foreign (Fifteenth Air Force) command.

On May 5, the USAAF launched 446 B-17s over Ploesti. JG 301 was engaged during the day and that night IV./NJG 6 clashed with RAF 205 Group Wellingtons and Halifaxes over the refineries. At 01:05 Kommandeur Lütje claimed his 33rd victory—Wellington "BL-R," LP191 of 40 Sqn was the first RAF bomber shot down over Romania and the first of several RAF Wellingtons that Lütje would add to his tally over Romania. Just as many Fortresses returned the next day; the RAF was active again at night.

When the intrusions calmed down, 2./NJG 100 resumed its long-range fighter missions, including over Sevastopol. But on May 31, massive bombing resumed and on June 4, 4./JG 301 arrived in Targsorul Nou. On June 9, during a powerful USAAF incursion, the Bf 110s were committed by day. At least five of them were shot down, including two Romanians (from 12./NJG 6). Alarmed by these losses, the FARR (Romanian Air Force) command forbade this unit to engage during the day.

Faced with overwhelming Allied superiority, the JGs and NJGs based in Romania fought all the harder as the Soviet front advanced westward. 4./JG 301 established itself at Targsorul and 6./JG 301 at Meri. On July 20, 1./ NJG 100 withdrew to Zilistea and 5./ NJG 200 left Nikolajew for Focsani.

On August 20, the Romanian–German front cracked under the pressure of two Soviet armies. On August 23, Romania changed sides and the Wehrmacht evacuated the country. On August 25, 11. and 12./NJG 6 carried out a final daytime operation before evacuating the next day for Hungary and then Schleissheim. IV./NJG 6 had fought vigorously against a far superior opponent. Its Kommandeur, Maj. Herbert Lütje, was credited with 10 victories during this period—seven Wellingtons, two P-38s, and one Il-2. Hptm. Ulrich von Meien, Staka of 2./NJG 100, downed three RAF Wellingtons, two on the night of May 7/8.

Two Staffeln appeared on the Eastern Front and in the Balkans during May/June—5./NJG 100 at Gross Beckereck (redesignated from 1./NJG 200) and 6./NJG 100 (ex-4./NJG 200) at Plovdiv-Krumowo. As a 4./NJG 100 already existed, a Stab II./NJG 100 was set up in June at Nisch with contributions from NJG 200. Hptm. Ulrich von Meien was named Kommandeur, but very little is known about the actions of this unit, which likely carried out anti-partisan actions, before withdrawing northward to avoid being surrounded in the Balkans. I./NJG 100 fell back to Poland and II./NJG 100 to Hungary. Around this time 5./NJG 200 became 7./NJG 100, but its location is unknown. Elsewhere, during July, a Nachtjagdstaffel Finnland/Norwegen was formed in the north at Lister.

Zur frommen Erinnerung im Gebete an

**Heinz Riederer**
Unteroffizier und K. O. B.

Inhaber des E. K. II in einem Nachtjagdgeschwader, ist nach Abschuß eines russischen Bombers bei einem Terrorangriff auf Tilsit im Alter von 23 Jahren gefallen.

Er wurde mit seinen Kameraden im Friedhof zu Heinrichswalde begraben.

Fr. Ant. Niedermayr, Regensburg

Although in principle a training unit, II./NJG 102 engaged aircraft at the front. On the night of August 27/28, 1944, the crew of Bf 110 G-4 coded "7J+EM" of 4./NJG 102 was shot down and killed after a victory over a Soviet bomber over Tilsit.

Bucharest-Otopeni. Hptm. Ulrich von Meien (left), then Staka of 2./NJG 100, and Hptm. Matin Bauer, Staka of 11./NJG 6. Both scored several victories over Romania.

A Ju 88 G-6 of I./NJG 100 coded "W7+LH" at Malacky (Slovakia) in early October 1944.

Ju 88 G-1 with the *Verbandskennung* "B4+DA" flown by an Ofw. Keilig from the Nachtjagdstaffel Finnland/Norwegen. This small "independent" Staffel was assigned to Luftflotte 5 before becoming 4./NJG 3 in 1945. Here the crew carry out a preflight inspection before a flight to Norway on October 7, 1944.

## I./NJG 100 in Poland, Summer–Fall 1944

By mid-1944, in a vain attempt to cover the ever-shifting and enormously long front lines, the crews of I./NJG 100 were operating from widely dispersed airfields over Poland. On the night of June 13/14 and guided by the night-fighting radar train *Sumatra I*, Ofw. Strohecker downed three Soviet bombers raiding Deblin (southeast of Warsaw) for his victories 8–10, while Fw. Herbert Simross of 1. Staffel also scored his tenth, downing four Il-4s southeast of Brest-Litovsk. On the night of June 17/18, flying an Fw 189 fitted with upward-firing MGs and guided by radar train *Sumatra III*, Lt. Gustav Francsi (1./NJG 100) shot down two "crabs" for his 17th and 18th *Luftsiege*. The term "crabs" was German pilot slang for the U-2 and R-5 biplanes employed to deliver and resupply partisans. Several I./NJG 100 aces achieved victories with what Oblt. Josef Pützkuhl called the "slowest night fighter in the world … we gave the Fw 189 antlers and *Schräge Musik* as MG 151s became available and hunted the R-5 and U-2 when there were no bombing raids—the Ju 88 was far too fast for these lame ducks." Lt. Helmut Konter of 3./NJG 100 flew a number of sorties in the Fw 189 and even had claims at the controls of an Fw 58. He achieved a triple U-2 *Abschuss* on the night of June 11/12 south of Orscha. Konter achieved 15 night victories in the East.

Leading Eastern Front night fighter ace Lt. Gustav Francsi carrying out preflight checks on an Fw 189. These twin-engine battlefield recce machines flew low and slow, hunting "crabs"—the antique Soviet biplanes used to service partisan groups behind the lines. (ECPA-D)

Lt. Gustav Francsi trained as a pilot late on, having flown over 100 missions with KG 40 as a flight engineer, claiming his first victory on the night of March 4/5, 1944, an Ilyushin DB-3 medium bomber. The location was reported as "Russia." With the launch of their huge summer offensive, *Bagration*, the Soviets stepped up their air operations at night while also continuing to land partisans behind the front. On June 28, Francsi downed a "B-24 Liberator" at 00:33 north of Baranovichi, downing a second "B-24" at 00:45—the two bombers were in fact Soviet Petlyakov Pe-8s of the ADD (long-range aviation). At 00:12 on June 29 Francsi accounted for an Ilyushin Il-4 for his 25th victory. Francsi continued his run of success during the summer of 1944, accounting for another Il-4 at 00:28 on July 1, three more on July 5, one at 00:00 on the night of July 8/9, and another at 23:48 on July 14.

Baranovichi, a long-term NJG 100 operating base, was retaken by the Soviets on July 8, 1944. This was glum news for the Kommandeur of I./NJG 100, Hptm. August Fischer, and his crews. A prewar Lufthansa pilot with over a million flight kilometers under his belt by the outbreak of war, Fischer had been an instructor at Blindflugschule 4 and served with the Fliegerstaffel des Führers (FdF), Hitler's private passenger airline. By the time he became a night fighter pilot serving with Wittgenstein on the Eastern Front in 1943, he was nearly 40. Fischer's first known victory was a Soviet Il-4 on the night of May 12/13, 1944, followed by an Il-2 on the night of June 17/18, 1944. He downed another Il-4 on the night of July 7/8, 1944. On the night of July 8/9, 1944, he shared three Il-4s with Fw. Düding and shared a fourth with Fw. Heinz de Vries on the night of July 9/10, 1944. Fischer recalled this period in his memoir:

> the front moved nearer and nearer. The advancing Russians were pushing our Würzburg radar trains back to areas from where they had set out when first deployed. Just five days ago, Oblt. Josef Pützkuhl (3./ NJG 100) had flown in from Pinsk … in only a few nights' operations he had downed some 20 enemy aircraft—in one night, six Russian machines had fallen to bursts from his slanting armament (July 5/6, 1944); only Wittgenstein had accomplished a similar feat on the Eastern Front prior to this exploit.

On August 1, 1944, the Polish Resistance began their uprising in Warsaw. *Bagration* had reached the outskirts of Warsaw, the Soviets outrunning their supply lines and exhausting their ground forces. The city and its railyards were of major importance to the Germans, and it was at this same moment that the Germans launched a wholly unexpected counterattack in front of Warsaw. This turn of events led to catastrophe for the Polish capital. The Poles began their uprising without any significant logistic reserves, assuming that the fighting would last only three days. The Red Army failed to intervene and the fighting lasted 63 days. The RAF and the USAAF attempted to mount hazardous and ultimately unsuccessful resupply operations. As one NJG 100 pilot put it, "the British come across the Carpathians from Italy with supplies for the bandits around Warsaw. We try and put a stop to this. And we succeed." Francsi claimed eight RAF bombers attempting to drop supplies over the Polish capital—including three "Lancasters" on the night of August 14/15 (all three were 178 Sqn B-24s from 205 Group). On the night of August 16/17 Francsi made four further claims: a Halifax over Opoczno at 23:53, another at Bochina, a "Lancaster" at Tarnów at 01:50, and another "Lancaster" at 02:18 over Przemyśl—part of a force of 18 "heavies." Once again three of his victims were in fact 205 Group Liberators. Another 1./NJG 100 ace, Ofw. Helmut

Dahms, claimed two more *Viermots* that night, the second at 02:27 near Kraków in the south, for his 15th and 16th *Luftsiege*. Francsi's success took his tally to 39 kills.

By November 1944, I./NJG 100 had moved north to Prowehren near Königsberg, East Prussia. 1. Staffel remained near Hohensalza. Francsi was awarded the Ritterkreuz on October 29, 1944. He claimed another Il-4 in an unknown location and an unknown time on the night of December 14/15, 1944. I./NJG 100 were also deployed on the night of November 20/21, the Soviets bombing the Latvian port of Vindava and the Lithuanian coastal city of Memel. Fellow night fighter ace Günther Bertram flying a 4./NJG 100 Ju 88 G-6 accounted for three Il-4s to reach his 27th out of 35 night victories, while Ofw. Helmut Dahms of 1./ NJG 100 claimed his 18th and 19th victories. Dahms ended the war with 28 *Abschüsse*. Lt. Francsi achieved his 42nd that night over an Il-4. On January 14/15, 1945 Francsi claimed his 43rd victory at an unrecorded time and location, while Oblt. Klaus Scheer, based nearby, claimed two PS-84s near Olyta to reach 22 victories.

At this stage of the war and in freezing temperatures relatively few night-interception fighter sorties were flown in the East, primarily because of fuel shortages. Those sorties that were flown comprised chiefly night ground-attack missions against the never-ending Soviet supply columns bringing up troops and equipment to the front. For example, Josef Pützkuhl flew only six sorties in the period late 1944 to early 1945, three night fighter and three night ground-attack sorties. His 26th and last victory was claimed as far back as July 25/26, 1944.

Lt. Gustav Francsi downed eight Allied *Viermots* over Warsaw on resupply sorties during August 1944. He is seen here on October 29, 1944, during the presentation ceremony for his Ritterkreuz. He achieved 59 *Abschüsse* and was the leading night fighter ace in the East. (via Theo Boiten)

# In the West: September 1944–January 1, 1945

After the evacuation of France and Romania, with retreat on all fronts, the Wehrmacht was clearly losing the war. The Nachtjagd was in a deplorable state and its decline as an effective arm accelerated after the Allied invasion of Normandy. The loss of forward airfields in France and Belgium, the poor standard of training received by replacement crews and the ever more acute shortage of fuel all contributed. A crying shortage of personnel was another factor. At this stage, there was little the Germans could do to reverse the decline.

An organization chart dated August 30, 1944 lists the NJ units involved in the Reichsverteidigung alone:

Leading *Wilde Sau Experte* Hptm. Friedrich-Karl Müller (1./NJGr.10) was awarded the Ritterkreuz on July 27, 1944. At the time he had 23 victories and shortly thereafter was appointed to command I./NJG 11. Müller's 24th victory on August 23, 1944 was his first (and likely only) Mosquito. His regular aircraft that summer was this Bf 109 G-6/AS "Red 2."

## In the West: September 1944–January 1, 1945

| | | | |
|---|---|---|---|
| Stab Gen.Kdo I. Jagdkorps | Trauenbrietzen | Stab/NJG 2 | Butzweilerhof (4/3) |
| - | | I./NJG 2 | Rothwesten (30/16) |
| Stab 1.Jagddivision | Döberitz | II./NJG 2 | Butzweilerhof (40/20) |
| Luftbeob. St. 1 | Neuruppin | II./NJG 3 | Gütersloh (20/19) |
| Kdo III./JG 300 | Jüterbog | III./NJG 3 | Düsseldorf (28/27) |
| | | III./NJG 4 | Twente (11/8) |
| Stab/NJG 5 | Parchim (1 a/c serviceable) | I./NJG 7 | Hanndorf (30/31) |
| NJGr 10 | Werneuchen (1/0) | Kdo I./NJG 7 | Rheine |
| 2./NJGr 10 | Finow (4/0) | Erpr.Kdo 410 | Venlo |
| 4./NJG 7 | Brieg (school unit) | Eins.Kdo NJGr 10 | Bonn/Rheine (38/37) |
| Stab/NJG 102 | Ohlau (school unit) | Stab/NJG 4 | Mainz-Finthen (0/0) |
| I./NJG 102 | Oels | I./NJG 4 | Langendiebach (28/0) |
| II./NJG 102 | Schönfeld-Seifersdorf | II./NJG 4 | Rhein-Main (21/9) |
| III./NJG 102 | Ohlau | III./NJG 2 | Langendiebach (36/31) |
| | | II./NJG 6 | Mainz-Finthen (26/21) |
| Stab Jafü Ostpreussen | Insterburg | | |
| I. and III./NJG 5 | Wormditt (15/13) | Stab 7. Jagddivision | Schleissheim |
| IV./NJG 5 | Powunden (21/21) | Luft.Beob. St. 7 | Echterdingen |
| Eins.St.NJG 102 | Powunden (6/6) | | |
| | | Stab/NJG 6 | Schleissheim (2/6) |
| Stab 2. Jagddivision | Stade | I./NJG 6 | Gross Sachsenheim/Hailfingen (44/34) |
| - | | IV./NJG 6 | Schleissheim (16/2) |
| Stab/NJG 3 | Stade (1/1) | II./NJG 5 | Hailfingen (27/14) |
| 1.+ 3./NJG 3 | Schleswig (25/22) | | |
| 2./NJG 3 | Nordholz | Stab NJG 101 | Ingolstadt (school unit) |
| IV./NJG 3 | Wittmundhafen/Varel (22/18) | I./NJG 101 | Ingolstadt |
| | | III./NJG 101 | Kitzingen (in training) |
| Stab 3. Jagddivision | Deelen | | |
| Luftbeob.St.2 | Eindhoven | Stab 8. Jagddivision | Wien-Cobenzl |
| Luftbeob.St.3 | Volkel | III./NJG 6 | Steinamanger/ Neusatz (32/22) |
| | | II./NJG 101 | Parndorf (school unit) |
| Stab/NJG 1 | Deelen (3/2) | Kdo Luftbeob. St. 7 | Zagreb/Villaorba |
| I./NJG 1 | Venlo (25/19) | | |
| II./NJG 1 | Deelen (43/25) | | |
| III./NJG 1 | Leeuwarden/Twente (40/23) | | |
| IV./NJG 1 | St.-Trond/Melsbroek (36/29) | | |

There were heavy losses of men and equipment during the fighting in Normandy. On September 7 at Sommesous, GIs found this train loaded with Bf 110 G-4 fuselages on rail wagons for transport back to Germany.

In other words, a total of some 676 fighter aircraft, of which 465 were combat-ready (not including NJG 100 and 200, which had been deployed outside the Reich but would return).

The transfer to East Prussia of three Gruppen of NJG 5 was explained by the recent attacks on Königsberg. III./NJG 101, which had become II./NJG 102 in December 1943, was reestablished on June 14, 1944 with new personnel and were also able to take on Soviet aircraft. On August 26, NJG 11 was set up, although it never had a Stab and was never a fully manned NJG. I./NJG 11 was led by Ritterkreuzträger Maj. Friedrich-Karl Müller, who had only the 1./NJG 11 at Lippstadt using elements of 6./JG 300 and 2./NJG 11 at Hangelar with contributions from 1./NJGr 10. These two Staffeln flew single-engine Fw 190/Bf 109s.

From that time onward, confident that it would face little opposition from a Tagjagd just as weak as the Nachtjagd, Bomber Command launched its four-engine bombers over the Reich by day (Emden, Castrop-Rauxel, etc.). In September, the Nachtjagd clashed with Bomber Command on eight occasions: on September 11/12, during an attack on Darmstadt by 240 bombers—12 were lost plus three others engaged in "gardening"—21 victories were claimed (including a Mosquito by Oblt. Kurt Welter). On September 12/13, Frankfurt am Main (with 387 aircraft) and Stuttgart (210 bombers) were the targets. There were 23 losses for 22 claims. On September 15/16, 490 bombers were unopposed in their attack on Kiel. On September 17, the Eichenlaub was awarded for his 58 *Abschüsse* to Hptm. Paul Zorner, this veteran leading III./NJG 5. On September 18/19, only two of the 206 Lancasters sent to Bremerhaven were lost, both probably claimed by Uffz. Hans Schadowski of 3./NJG 3 (his 11th and 12th confirmed). On September 19/20, 22 bombers were sent to Münchengladbach/Rheydt losing six aircraft (eight were claimed by six pilots). On September 23/24, a massive attack by 549 four-engine bombers on Neuss was backed up by 136 Lancasters on the Dortmund–Ems Canal. Twenty-one aircraft were lost. A 22nd was lost when 113 aircraft bombed the Handorf airfield. Fifteen victories were awarded to the NJ. Hptm. Hermann Greiner (11./NJG 1) achieved his 40th victory, while Hptm. Schnaufer (Kdr of IV./NJG 1) was credited with four *Abschüsse* (95th–98th). On September 27/28, the NJ downed just one of the 227 aircraft that bombed Kaiserslautern. It was the 48th *Luftsieg* returned by Maj. Hans-Joachim Jabs, leading NJG 1, but five NJ twins fell victim to Mosquitos (with only one survivor). On the night of September 28/29, Bomber Command set up traps to entice the Nachtjäger into the air, where they could be picked off by Mosquitos. This was the case for the Ju 88 G of Hptm. Fritz Söthe (4./NJG 4), holder of 18 victories, who was killed. Söthe had already been hit by a Mosquito over France on June 11/12, 1944, but was only wounded.

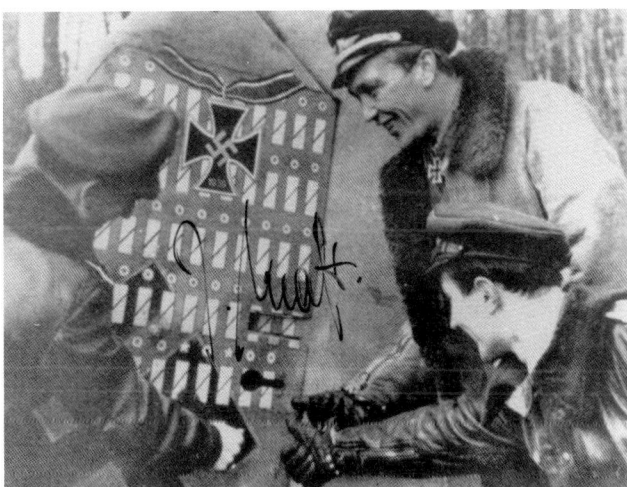

Oblt. Josef Kraft and crew (left, gunner Papst and radio operator Täubner) admiring their elaborate victory scoreboard following the painting of a 49th kill marking on the tailfin of the Austrian ace's 7./NJG 6 Bf 110 G-4—note *Abschüsse* 38–39 (fourth row down, obscured by Kraft's signature) which were red stars while victories 40 and 41 (fifth row, hidden) were also Soviet Li transports (a copy of the American DC-3). The white stars are B-24s (although RAF machines). Kraft flew some of his first combat sorties with I./NJG 4 at Florennes during July 1943 where he had been sent by his Kommandeur (Schoenert, II./NJG 5) " to get my first victories."

The death of Helmut Lent in a crash came as a shock to the entire Luftwaffe. Hermann Göring attended his funeral. His obituary notice stated that Lent was undefeated (*unbesiegt*).

Three Ritterkreuze were awarded on the 30th: to Austrian Oblt. Josef Kraft, Staka of 7./NJG 6, for his 44 victories; to Hptm. Werner Husemann, leading I./NJG 3, for his 30 victories; and to Ofw. Johannes Richter, Rudolf Schoenert's radio/gunner, for his participation in 61 victories.

Bomber Command continued its day raids (Walcheren, Bergen, etc.) without any real losses, while regularly employing its Mosquitos. As T. Boiten points out, the Luftwaffe's fuel crisis had reached a critical point—it was mostly only the *Experten* that were sent up to counter incoming raids. Some young crews were still being committed of course but only in small numbers. In September some 800 sorties were flown, for a desultory 34 claims.

The next month, the first "serious" contact with the Nachtjagd took place on the night of October 4/5 when 78 aircraft mined the Kattegat and Oslo. Three were shot down by NJG 3. Nachtjagd losses in October amounted to a further 54 aircraft and crews. Losses included Obstlt. Helmut Lent, Kommodore of NJG 3 and victor in 110 air combats, who suffered an engine failure on landing on Paderborn on October 5. In the ensuing crash, Lent and his crew were so severely injured that they all died within the next two days. During his last 46 night sorties, Lent had scored 38 victories, testament to his exceptional talent as a

Horst Henning celebrates a milestone flight with his KG 77 comrades. As a Ritterkreuzträger, he transferred to the Nachtjagd during 1944 but was KIA on the night of October 7/8.

night fighter. Another Ritterkreuzträger perished with Lent, his radio operator Ofw. Walter Kubisch. Also on board was war reporter Werner Kark.

On October 6/7, during a double attack on Dortmund and Bremen, four bombers and three Mosquitos were shot down (including two Mosquitos by young airmen). Nachtjäger were also used on so-called free-hunting operations, a throwback to the *Fernnachtjagd* of 1940/41. On the night of October 6/7, several NJG 1 crews set off for Belgium, losing at least four of their number: after taking off from Düsseldorf, the aircraft of Fw. Robert Koch (5./NJG 1) suffered an engine problem. The aircraft was then attacked (by a Mosquito or a Black Widow) and the crew bailed out over Peer. Under interrogation as a POW, Koch said he had operated from St.-Trond in 1943, having been wounded in daylight combat on October 14 that year. He was credited with five victories. A second Bf 110 G-4 of 5./NJG 1 was hit by flak over Belgium. Its pilot was able to bring it back to his lines near Aachen and gave the order to bail out. Only one of the crew was recovered. The four crewmembers flying in the Ju 88 G-1 of Uffz. Albert Kurzec (11./NJG 1) were killed when the machine crashed at Amay. These missions seem to have been carried out mainly over Belgium and the Netherlands to slow the Allied advance.

On the night of October 7/8, the Ju 88 G-1 flown by Oblt. Horst Henning (8./NJG 3) crashed for an undetermined reason at Hadersleben (Denmark). Henning, previously a bomber pilot with 1./KG 77, had been awarded the Ritterkreuz in 1942. Transferred to the Nachtjagd in the summer of 1944, he shot down six bombers in July/August.

Bochum was bombed by 435 aircraft on the night of October 9/10. Three *Experten* scored four victories—including the 99th and 100th for Hptm. Schnaufer and the 10th for his future brother-in-law, Oblt. Georg Fengler. On October 14, 1,063 aircraft attacked Duisburg and, the following night (14th/15th), a further 1,005 returned to the city. A young crew claimed a Mosquito and Lt. Arnold Döring (7./NJG 2), future Ritterkreuzträger, his 20th victory, over a *Viermot*.

Fw. Oskar Maag, a pilot in 1./NJG 3, was KIA on October 14/15, shot down by one of the numerous RAF Mosquitos in the air over Schleswig.

Three comrades, three Ritterkreuzträger ... from left: Gänsler, Schnaufer, and Rumpelhardt. After the war, Gänsler was unable to return home and, like Fengler, was taken on by Schnaufer in the family business in Calw.

On October 15/16, Wilhelmshaven was the target for the night. Boiten points out that although this was only a brief penetration into Germany, Bomber Command adopted an elaborate scheme of routing and deception tactics to protect the force. The RAF still feared the Nachtjagd, even though it had been reduced to its simplest expression. Six *Viermots* were credited to six pilots, including three aces. On October 16, Schnaufer was awarded the Diamonds for his 100 victories. On November 1, he took command of NJG 4. On the 18th, Lt. Kurt Welter of 10./JG 300, a specialist *Moskito-Jagd* Staffel, was awarded the Ritterkreuz for his 34 victories (including eight Mosquitos).

On October 19/20, Bomber Command attacked Stuttgart and Nuremberg with 800 bombers. Five victories were achieved by the NJ but only one by an ace, Hptm. Heinz Rökker (2./NJG 2). By late October the Nachtjagd was hardly involved at all. On October 27, I./NJG 11 finally received a full complement of single-engine fighters with the establishment of a 3./NJG 11 at Hangelar. On the 30th, for some unknown reason, IV./NJG 3 became III./NJG 2, a new IV./NJG 3 being formed from the old III./NJG 2. I./NJG 7 became IV./NJG 2. The previous day, in addition to Francsi, Ritterkreuze were awarded to Maj. Walter Borchers, Kommodore of NJG 5 and member of ZG 76 at the start of the war, for his 45 victories; Oblt. Wilhelm Johnen, Staka of 8./NJG 6, for his 33 victories, including four Soviet aircraft (shortly afterward he took command of III./NJG 6); and Ofw. Hans-Georg Schierholz, radio operator in Rudolf Frank's crew (killed in April) and then in Werner Husemann's. He took part in 54 victories but had to bail out on four occasions.

On November 1/2, 288 bombers attacked Oberhausen, four failing to return. Eight victories were awarded to the Nachtjagd. On November 2/3, almost 1,000 bombers flew to Düsseldorf and the Luftwaffe was able to restore its reputation by inflicting 19 losses for some 40 victory claims. This overclaim is probably attributable to several factors, most notably individual bombers—despite damage—staying airborne and being attacked by several night fighters in the clear conditions. Maj. Paul Semrau (II./NJG 2) claimed four

Wilhelm Johnen's career was not hampered by his internment in Switzerland, as he was awarded the Ritterkreuz on October 29, 1944.

(his 33rd–36th), while Ofw. Wilhelm "Willi" Morlock and his Funker Fw. Alfred Soika (3./NJG 1) accounted for six (his 11th–16th) and claimed a probable seventh, all south of Düsseldorf between 19:25 and 19:37—the highest number of kills claimed on a single He 219 sortie. Two further He 219 pilots claimed their first victories: Oblt. Ruppert Thurner (3./NJG 1) and Uffz. Werner Wollenhaupt (2./NJG 1).

On November 4/5, Bochum and the Dortmund–Ems Canal were attacked by 1,000 bombers. Over Bochum, the Luftwaffe (NJ/Flak) proved once again that it could still fight back, even on a small scale, as 28 bombers were lost (including five from Elvington's 346 (French) Sqn). A further three were shot down near the canal. Claims of 38 aircraft were not too exaggerated. Although five young pilots opened their score—including two for Lt. Jurgen Prietze of 3./NJG 1—the *Experten* filed numerous claims: Hptm. Hermann Greiner (IV./NJG 1) downed two while Oblt. Hans-Heinz Augenstein (12./NJG 1) and Hptm. Heinz Rökker (2./NJG 2) each claimed three. Around 10 NJ twins were shot down, most of them by Mosquitos—the machines of 100 Group had one of their best nights of the war, downing four Ju 88s and three Bf 110s. Almost certainly one of their victims was Willi Morlock, the successful 3./NJG 1 pilot from the night of the 2nd/3rd. His He 219 coded "G9+HL" (WNr. 190182) crashed at Ibbenbüren. Radio operator Soika safely ejected from the stricken machine. Morlock's score stood at 16—in reality it was probably less than 10 *Luftsiege*, although he was likely still one of the leading He 219 aces.

On November 6/7, ground controllers were surprised by some 400 aircraft flying toward the Mitteland Canal and Koblenz. Nevertheless, 12 Lancasters were lost, 11 of which were attributed to the NJ (including 10 to six aces). On November 11/12, Bomber Command concentrated on Hamburg and Dortmund, losing seven of the 450 or so bombers involved. Eight *Luftsiege* were awarded, including two to young crews who opened their score.

In the days that followed, the RAF sent its bombers during the day over the battleship *Tirpitz* (November 12), over Dortmund (November 13), and in support of the U.S. Army over the Rhine (November 16). On November 21/22 a new confrontation with the NJ took place over Aschaffenburg and Castrop-Rauxel—six of the 550 *Viermots* were shot down, 12 being awarded to the NJ.

On November 23, III./NJG 101, reformed in June, was disbanded as this school unit had become redundant. On November 25, Fw. Heinrich Wilke (II./NJG 100), Paul Zorner's regular radio operator, was awarded the Ritterkreuz for his part in 58 victories. The night of

Lt. Otto Fries (2./NJG 1) was credited with two Lancasters (victories 12–13) during the night of November 6//, 1944. He was one of those little-known aces who scored at regular intervals and survived the war.

November 26/27 was typical of the NJ's skirmishes with Bomber Command operating on special missions. That night, two Stirlings carrying SOE agents flew to Denmark. One was shot down at Juist by Hptm. Dietrich Kornblum, a 9./NJG 2 Ritterkreuzträger from KG 53. Unfortunately for him, his victim exploded and blew his Ju 88 apart. The second Stirling was intercepted by Maj. Husemann, another RK ace, leading I./NJG 3. A skilled gunner destroyed the Ju 88's engines and wounded the radio operator, Ofw. Schierholz (another Ritterkreuzträger), and Husemann had to make an emergency landing.

On November 27, Nachtjagdstaffel Finnland/Norwegen was redesignated Nachtjagdstaffel Norwegen. 4./NJG 7 was incorporated into the Schulstaffel/NJG 3 and, despite the difficulties of the moment, a II./NJG 11 (Hptm. Martin Finkeldey) was set up at Jüterbog with the support of 10./JG 300 (but probably with only a handful of single-engine aircraft).

The beginning of December was a continuation of November, with very few Nachtjagd claims. On December 4/5, however, in an attack on Karlsruhe and Heilbronn, 13 Lancasters were lost out of a force of over 800 bombers—11 were attributed to the NJ, including three to Lt. Peter Spoden (Stab II./NJG 6). Thirteen bombers were also lost on December 6/7 during three raids on Leuna, Osnabrück, and Giessen. Some 1,100 four-engine bombers were involved, with 18 claimed by the NJ, but only half a dozen could be confirmed.

## In Profile:
## Kurt Welter—Nachtjagd Jet Ace?

By the late summer and fall of 1944 only one Staffel of the original *Wilde Sau* Geschwader was flying single-engine night fighters—10.(N)/JG 300. This unit specialized in *Moskito*-hunting and had been established to combat the almost-nightly incursions flown by Mosquito bombers of the RAF's LNSF. Operating out of Jüterbog south of Berlin, under Staffelkapitän Hptm. Boettcher, 10. Staffel flew a modified *Wilde Sau* system— guided by two vertical searchlight beams and a ground controller, the unit's high performance Bf 109 G-14/AS fighters loitered at high altitude—10,000 meters—above the corridors used by the Mosquitos ranging with quasi-impunity over northern Germany and making increasingly frequent incursions over Berlin. One notable pilot of this Staffel was Kurt Welter who claimed several Mosquitos downed during August and September 1944 and who was awarded the RK in October 1944. Not that this explains why a "lowly" Luftwaffe Oberleutnant flying in the *Wilde Sau* was given a Staffel of the new Me 262 jets. It was perhaps because of the desperation gripping the Luftwaffe hierarchy. East German author Manfred Jurleit writing in the 1980s relates how "in early July 1944 the Chief of Staff of I. Jagdkorps, Oberst Heiner Wittmer, met a young Leutnant from JG 300, Kurt Welter, who had come up with an unusual idea. He urged the Oberst to consider putting the Me 262 into service as a *Wilde Sau* night fighter. Wittmer subsequently spoke to his commander Beppo Schmidt who contacted Luftflotte Reich CO, Generaloberst Stumpf, who spoke to von Brauchitsch, Chef Adjutant, and Göring himself. A *Führerbefehl* subsequently gave the green light and Welter—now an Oberleutnant—retrained on the Me 262 in Lechfeld."

Between November 1944 and January 1945 Welter was the only pilot of the so-called Kommando Welter and he effectively pioneered night-fighting in the Me 262. His Kommando was officially designated 10./NJG 11 on January 25, 1945 with a typical Staffel-strength establishment of 12 Me 262s—an additional fourth Staffel attached to II./NJG 11. By this time Welter had been joined by a small group of experienced night fighter pilots, most of whom he invited personally into the unit. One of these was Fw. Karl-Heinz Becker who recalled:

> The first attempts at night-fighting in Me 262 jets took place during November 1944. Welter had trialed night interceptions over Berlin flying out of Rechlin-Lärz in a single-seat Me 262. He would land at airfields around Greater Berlin at the end of his sortie and fly back to Lärz during the day. He achieved several victories during these flights. At the time I was at Strausberg with the Ergänzungsgruppe für Tagjagd, the day fighter operational training wing, on a conversion course after coming from heavy night fighters, but after a phone call from Welter on December

13, 1944, I joined him at Rechlin-Lärz. It was here that the [jet night-fighting] Staffel was being established and in January we moved to Burg (near Magdeburg, southwest of Berlin). It was from here that we flew our first night jet-training sorties and from mid-February 1945 the first sharp combat flights.

March 1945 was the most successful and busiest month for Welter and his handful of pilots. The night of March 27/28 was significant for the first nocturnal sortie of the Me 262 B-1a/U1—the radar-equipped twin-seat Me 262. "Red 12" was flown by Lt. Herbert Altner and his radio operator, Uffz. Reinhard Lommatzsch until their engine flamed out when "Red 12" was lost and Lommatzsch killed.

Despite the overblown claims made for 10./NJG 11 and the (internet) myths and stories, a detailed documentary analysis of RAF Bomber Command Mosquito attrition during 1945 shows that "only a maximum of 15 Mosquitos, out of a total of around 94 lost to all causes between February and April 1945, could have been shot down at night by 10./NJG 11." (Rod Mackenzie in the *Nachtjagd War Diaries*.)

"Red 10" was a rare radar-equipped twin-seat Me 262 B-1a/U1 on the strength of 10./NJG 11. The handful of twin-seat Me 262s actually delivered were conversions from single-seaters.

GIs pose in front of the tailfin of Ju 88 WNr. 710891, coded "3C+HM" of 4./NJG 4 lost at an undetermined location on December 23/24, 1944. The photo was taken around February 1945.

# Wacht am Rhein

On December 16, the German army launched *Wacht am Rhein*, an offensive aimed at the port of Antwerp. Most of the fighting took place in Belgium and eastern France. The Luftwaffe engaged no fewer than 17 Gruppen from the NJGs 1, 2, 3, 4, 5, and 6 in *Nachtschlachteinsätze*—night ground-attack sorties—as in Normandy, where the results had hardly been convincing. Night fighters without ground control were sent deep into the Allied lines to strafe and bomb military encampments, vehicle columns traveling with lights on, rail convoys, etc. This meant inexperienced pilots operating in Allied airspace, in complete darkness and at very low altitude. Although Allied flak could be dangerous, the risks of hitting trees, pylons, or buildings were far greater.

Several Ju 88s and Bf 110s disappeared. Capture reports, however, give details of the fate of some crews. December 23/24: Ju 88 G-1 of 4./NJG 2 had taken off separately from Vechta to patrol the Netherlands and the coast; attacked by a Mosquito, it was landed at Hasselt (three prisoners). Ju 88 G-1 of 4./NJG 4 crashed at Heer-sur-Meuse (three killed). Ju 88 G-1 of 4./NJG 4 failed to return from a *Nachtschlacht* sortie (three missing). December 25/26: Bf 110 G-4 of 8./NJG 1 shot down by American flak at Grandhan (one killed, two prisoners). December 26/27: Ju 88 G-6 of 9./NJG 2—six aircraft of 9./NJG 2 left Broekzetel to join seven 7. Staffel Ju 88s (from Jever) at Handorf, and attacked rail convoys in the Calais region. Two locomotives were targeted by the crew of "4R+ET," attempting to use up their remaining ammunition in the Brussels sector but were forced to return by antiaircraft fire. Damaged, it was shot down at Verviers by a Black Widow (three prisoners). Ju 88 G-6 of 4./NJG 2 crashed at Namur (two killed, two prisoners). Ju 88 G-1 of 8./NJG 4 was shot down at Warampage (two prisoners, one killed—Oblt. Walter Riedelberger, Staka and ace with nine victories).

The few Gruppen not involved in *Schlacht* sorties continued to fight on over the Reich, but their successes were limited and the brunt of the defensive actions fell to the Flak. In the now-hopeless fighting, losses increased as the Mosquitos continued to hunt down the NJ twins. On the night of December 24/25, Hptm. and Eichenlaubträger Heinz Strüning (9./NJG 1) was shot down near Bergisch-Gladbach. He bailed out but hit one of the tailfins of his Bf 110 G-4. The body of this 56-victory ace—his tally included two Mosquitos—was not found until two months later. Like III./NJG 101 in November, the recently formed III./NJG 102 was disbanded in December. These training units had become redundant.

Wreck of a Ju 88 of NJG 4 shot down at Jarny (France) on the evening of December 24, 1944.

Jakob Granderath, a pilot with 5./NJG 3, was one of the airmen lost with their crew "over southern Belgium." His obituary notice states that he was a transport pilot in the Mediterranean in 1942/43.

On the night of December 27/28, a IV./NJG 2 Ju 88 G-6 coded "4R+NU" engaged on a strafing sortie (*Nachtschlachteinsatz*), attacked a column of American vehicles near Beaumont (Belgium). It flew so low that it hit treetops and crashed at Grandrieu.

In the West: September 1944–January 1, 1945

On December 17, 1944, Bf 110 coded "2Z+IV" of 11./NJG 6 took off from Kitzingen at around 13:00 for a training flight. The crew was "bounced" and shot down in flames by Maj. James Dalglish (354th FG). The pilot was killed but his two crew were able to bail out.

A Ju 88 of 11./NJG 3 at Grove.

In the early hours of January 1, 1945, American flak at Palenberg shot down the Ju 88 G-6 flown by Uffz. Franz Josef Schulte (5./NJG 2) on a *Nachtschlachteinsatz*. The three crewmen—here in front of a Ju 88 C—were captured. Schulte had a victory to his credit, which was in the process of being confirmed.

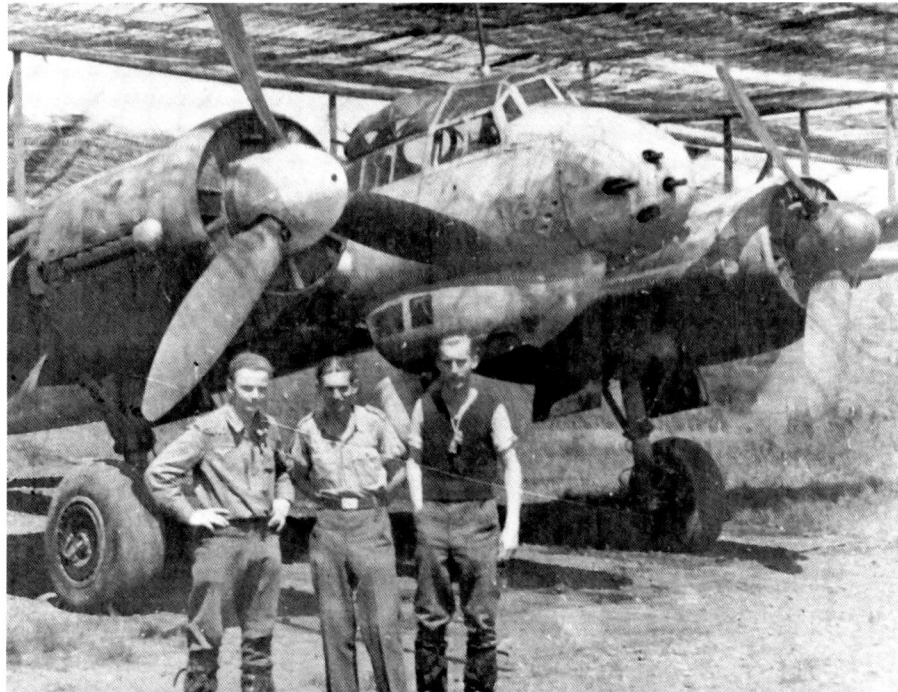

103

# Extracts From Interrogations of Nachtjagd POWs Captured on the Last Night of 1944

a) Three miles northeast of Hasselt, January 1, 1945, 0h15. Bf 110 G-6 of 4./NJG 1

An aircraft of 4. Staffel and an unknown number of aircraft of other Staffeln took off from Varel on December 31 to attack railway lines in the Hasselt sector. This aircraft flew at low altitude and strafed a train. But before it could spot any other interesting targets, it was hit by light antiaircraft fire at a height of 50 meters. The pilot crashed but was killed; the radio operator and machine gunner were captured.

b) Southeast of Mechelen, December 31, 1944, 23:45. Ju 88 G coded "4R+GU" of 10./NJG 2

The entire crew was killed. A night fighter is believed to have been responsible for the crash.

c) Southeast of Brussels, December 31, 1944, 23.30 hrs. Ju 88 G-6 coded "D5+EN" of 5./NJG 3

Some 18 5. and 6./NJG 3 machines took off from Schleswig to attack road and rail traffic in Belgium. The flight was to Hamburg and then directly to the target. The aircraft taking part in the raid had had their radar equipment dismantled to prevent it falling into enemy hands. The D5+EN therefore no longer had an SN-2. While flying at around 2,000 meters, it was attacked by a Mosquito and three crew bailed out, including the pilot, Lt. Gerhard Schmalen, Staffelführer of 5./NJG 3.

d) Near Huy, January 1, 1945, 2.30 am. Ju 88 G-1 coded "D5+CL" of 7./NJG 3

Around four aircraft from 7./NJG 3 took off from Stade to attack traffic in Belgium. At 23:00 on December 31, the crews received their instructions. The pilot maintained an altitude of 2,000 meters, then descended to 50 meters to cross the front line near Aix. He then stabilized at 100/150 meters while the crew searched for a target. But the aircraft was hit by light antiaircraft fire and the crew (except for the radio operator) bailed out. None of the aircraft was equipped with upward-firing cannon; the prisoner reports that this type of weapon is becoming unpopular with crews as it is thought to interfere with the *Mutterkompass* (main compass). Some recently captured night-fighting crews complained that their compass had been playing tricks on them.

e) Twenty miles south of Liège, December 31, 1944, around 23:00. Ju 88 G-6 coded "D5+PT" of 9./NJG 3

Six or seven aircraft of 9./NJG 3 took off from Ütersen to attack traffic in the Liège sector. The entire III./NJG 3 was committed. G-6 "D5+PT" flew from Ütersen to the Ida signal beacon before setting course for Liège at an altitude of 300 meters. Shortly before crossing the front line, the pilot climbed to 1,500 meters and then returned to a much lower altitude. Near Verviers, the aircraft followed a rail line and spotted a train. But it was then hit by a burst of antiaircraft fire, forcing the crew to abandon the machine.

(Note the different tactics used to cross the front line: either at low or high altitude)

## *Bodenplatte*

On January 1, 1945, the Luftwaffe launched Operation *Bodenplatte*. This daylight attack on Allied airfields in France, Belgium, and the Netherlands was too late to make any difference to the situation. Although it destroyed a large number of Allied aircraft, the number of Tagjagd pilots lost sealed its fate: 143 pilots killed and missing, 70 captured, and 21 wounded, the largest single-day loss for the Luftwaffe.

Oblt. August Györy had been awarded his RK in 4.(F)/122. Killed in Belgium on New Year's Eve, he is said to have made around 30 flights in the Nachtjagd without winning any victories.

The last night of 1944 saw a great deal of activity by the Nachtjagd (see textbox). It was during these operations that Austrian Oblt. August Györy's Ju 88 G-1 went missing. Györy had been awarded the Ritterkreuz for competent flying with 4.(F)/122 on various fronts (including the Mediterranean). His Ju 88 reportedly came down between Brussels and Antwerp.

In the early hours of January 1, 1945, Ju 88s served as guides (*Lotse*) for Tagjagd formations often made up of fledgling pilots unable to find their way around. The *Lotse* pilots must have been instructors, because at least two aircraft from II./NJG 101 were lost to flak in Belgium. The crew of Fw. Günther Kotschote, guiding II./JG 4, was captured. His superior wrote to his wife:

> Your husband did not return from a mission on January 1, 1945 and has been reported missing. According to the officer commanding the fighter unit, your husband was on a mission against an enemy airfield near Liège. The front was crossed at low altitude and at 9.05 am the formation came under heavy flak fire near Aywaylle. Your husband's aircraft was hit in the left engine, which caught fire. The plane hit the ground and was destroyed. We have no information about the fate of the crew.

The other NJG 101 crew perished at Vielsalm.

# Terminal Decline: January–May 1945

The Nachtjagd was in terminal decline. Although victories were still being racked up, losses continued to mount. On the night of January 5/6, 1945, 664 bombers attacked Hanover, losing 31 of their number. Thirty victories were claimed by the NJ, half of which could be confirmed. Gkr. I./NJG 1 Werner Baake downed three Halifax "heavies"—his last three claims of the war. Modrow claimed his 33rd *Abschuss*—and last—of the war.

On the night of January 6/7, three of 629 bombers were lost over Hanau and Neuss. Among those NJ killed was Hptm. Alfons Köster, a former I./NJG 2 long-range night fighter ace with 26 victories who had taken part in the *Fernnachtjagd* in 1940/41 and who had been awarded the Ritterkreuz for his 16 victories over England and Africa. Staka of 12./NJG 3, he hit a house while landing at Varel and was killed with his crew.

On January 12, the Red Army launched a powerful offensive. Fuel and flak guns were sent east as a priority and Luftwaffe activity in the West was severely impacted. The German offensive through the Ardennes petered out and the forces deployed fell back.

On the night of February 3/4 some 341 Lancasters hit hydrogenation plants in the Ruhr. Twelve were lost—only 3 percent of the force. The He 219s of I./NJG 1 claimed two including the 39th for Kommandeur and Hptm. Werner Baake, a 100 Sqn machine that came down near Venlo. Another I./NJG 1 pilot to apparently score was Hptm. Alexander Graf Rességuier de Miremont, who returned his first *Abschuss* flying the He 219. Rességuier had been an original member of JG Herrmann and was an experienced night fighter pilot (three kills in JG 300 and NJG 5). His victim that night is not known with certainty, but in the exchange of fire Rességuier's He 219 (WNr.290070, coded "G9+OH") was also hit, the crew successfully deploying their ejection seats. Rességuier landed safely by parachute near Kempen while his Funker Fw. Fritz Habicht (previously teamed with Nabrich) came down in tall trees and was injured.

Hptm. Hans Krause received the RK on February 7, 1945. Among other feats he was credited with five Soviet bombers downed. In total, 26 of his claims were confirmed, three with 1./NJG 3 (October 1942–March 1943) and 23 with 6./NJG 101 (February–November 1944). His gunner claimed a Mosquito on March 4, 1945, returning from *Gisela* with the Stab I./NJG 4 but Krause's Ju 88 G-6 (3C+BC) was heavily damaged in the encounter and crash-landed at Hamm. Krause was NJG 101's top scorer. (via Matthews)

Habicht had 17 *Abschussbeteiligungen* (victory participations). Meanwhile Fw. Günther Thurow was forced to belly-land his damaged He 219 (WNr. 290058, coded "G9+VH") at Münster-Handorf after being attacked by a Mosquito and a third He 219 crash-landed and burst into flames (damage assessed at 60 percent).

On February 7, Hptm. Hans Krause, leading I./NJG 4, was awarded the Ritterkreuz for his 28 victories (at least 10 still unconfirmed by March 1945), including five Soviet bombers. Months earlier, Krause had led 6./NJG 101, which had been sent to Central Europe in September 1944 and had clashed with both the Red Army and the Western Allies. On November 17, he had even flown an armed reconnaissance over southern Italy, shooting down two Halifaxes near Cape Ancona.

As the victories dwindled, a depleted Nachtjagd continued to lose crews young and old. On February 8, Hptm. Paul Semrau, Kommodore of NJG 2, was returning to land at Twente after a daytime test flight when he was surprised by a Spitfire which shot down his Ju 88 G-6, killing the entire crew. He was posthumously awarded the rank of Major and the Eichenlaub. The night of February 13/14 saw the terrible bombing of Dresden and the apparent gratuitous destruction of a great city. There were only two victories for the Nachtjagd—both claimed by Maj. Hans Leickhart (II./NJG 5), his 11th and 12th. The following night, during the bombing of Chemnitz and Rositz, the Nachtjäger were credited with 15 victories for 17 bombers actually lost out of the 950 or so engaged. They were awarded to aces with at least five victories.

On February 19, Bavarian Ofw. Anton "Balbo" Hörwick was killed near Königsberg when his Ju 88 G-6 was shot down by Soviet fighters. Hörwick had fought in Spain with K/88 of the Condor Legion before transferring to KG 2 and KG 3. He was awarded the Ritterkreuz on August 8, 1944 while serving with I./NJG 7 (later IV./NJG 2). His unit, sent east in 1945, was mainly involved in ground-support missions. On the night of February 21/22, during a combined attack on Duisburg, Worms, and the Mitteland Canal, Bomber Command lost 34 aircraft, 57 of which were credited to the Nachtjagd, including seven to Ofw. Günther Bahr,

During their advance, Allied troops came across several downed Bf 110s.

A Ju 88 of I./NJG 4 seen on a daytime test flight.

10 to Maj. Schnaufer, and five to Maj. Max Eckhoff (a former KG 55 pilot transferred to the Stab II./NJG 2). Three young pilots opened their score.

On February 28, Hptm. Walter Engel was awarded the Ritterkreuz. In May 1940, he had flown with 4.(F)/14 and then moved on to KG 3 and 4. In May 1944 he was retrained as a Nachtjäger and became Staka of 3./NJG 5 before being promoted to Kommandeur of I./NJG 5. This Gruppe was based in East Prussia and Engel was credited with 10 victories, nine of his claims Soviet aircraft.

## *Gisela* and Nachtschlacht

Operation *Gisela* has fascinated historians, even though for the Nachtjagd it was nothing more than a poor copy of Operation *Bodenplatte*, the swansong of the Tagjagd. This idea is said to have been the brainchild of General "Beppo" Schmid, who was not an aviator, but probably accepted by a good number of crews depressed by the decline of the Nachtjagd. Some 80 fighters from NJG 2, III. and IV./NJG 3, NJG 4, and III./NJG 5 flew to England on the night of March 3/4 to hunt RAF bombers returning from a raid over Germany.

Lt. Arnold Döring (10./ NJG 3)—a former bomber pilot with 9./KG 53 and *Wilde Sau* night fighter with JG 300—had taken off for *Gisela* from Wittmundhafen at the controls of "D5+FV" and claimed two RAF bombers shot down over Yorkshire.

> By now my fuel was getting low and it was time to think about swinging onto a heading for home. I made a last circuit of the aerodrome identified as Dishforth but, as the moon had slipped behind a bank of cloud, we were unable to make out any further targets. However, we were still some 80 kilometers from the coast. We were under instructions to return with empty magazines in our nose weapons and had been given free rein to strafe any ground targets. The enemy didn't hesitate to shoot at anything that moved on the ground by day over Germany—road traffic, trains, people working in fields or going about their business in villages and towns. Now he would get a taste of his own medicine. A double Morse identification beacon ahead of me served as target practice and was quickly destroyed. A train heading northward, lights blazing, was singled out for a long burst. Several wagons were set alight. Copious amounts of steam issued from the many impact strikes on the loco. I emptied my last rounds into the streets of Scarborough itself before emerging over the sea. I quickly let down over the waves and suddenly found myself in the middle of a convoy assembling off the coast. A searchlight probed the night skies, illuminating a barrage balloon that was immediately hoisted down, while Paul fired off a red flare, the international emergency signal. We avoided

the balloon—thanking our British hosts below—before setting course for home just meters above the rolling waves of the North Sea. We had enjoyed great good fortune, taken the British completely by surprise, achieved two victories ourselves and caused great confusion if the other downings we had witnessed were anything to go by.

*Gisela* was the last realization of the fantasy of "successful" Nachtjäger intrusions into British airspace. According to one source, had German intruder operations been maintained over Britain in 1941 and thereafter, the British night-flying training program could have been halted or disrupted. This omission could be regarded as one of "the major errors made by the OKL concerning the air defense of Germany." If these historians had seriously studied the ratio of losses to successes of I./NJG 2 in 1940/41, they would have quickly understood that this tactic carried out with few resources (a reinforced Gruppe) was a clear failure. The Luftwaffe did not have enough aircraft in 1941 to carry out a large-scale intrusion campaign. And it had even fewer in 1945, its manpower resources skeletal.

The RAF's official history states that "approximately 200 fighters were involved." According to General Marcel Noirot:

> On Saturday March 3, the enemy changed tactics. I was not one of the 28 French crews who took off from Elvington for Kamen. The return journey was uneventful … except that intruders were reported in the stream. So it was with relief that we saw our planes arrive over the airfield. The moon was shining and in the misty light we could see the silhouettes of Ju 88s chasing our planes, some of which were running out of fuel and had to make emergency landings. The ineffective flak was firing at everything that flew. Lieutenant Terrien of 347 Sqn was at 2,000 feet over Elvington when he suddenly saw the airfield lights go out and at the same time received orders to move away as quickly as possible. He immediately switched off his position lights, but too late. He had been spotted by an intruder who shot him down in the immediate vicinity of the airfield. The plane was in flames but, like any good pilot, Terrien remained at the controls to allow his comrades to jump. Second Lieutenant Laucou of the 347th suffered the same fate when he took refuge at another airfield and was killed along with his mechanic.

Twenty-seven years after the event, Noirot wrote: "On the bomber side, losses were extremely severe although they were not revealed. There was talk of 100 Halifaxes being shot down, but there was no confirmation." In reality, Bomber Command's losses were around 15 Halifaxes and 12 Lancasters. Two Mosquitos were lost, one of which presumably fell in combat. Nine aircraft were listed as damaged. However, rumors prove that *Gisela* caused quite a stir in the RAF and that its impact was more psychological than material. On the German side, 23 fighters were lost, three of which crashed in England. According to Noirot: "For the Luftwaffe, it was a suicide mission. Like the aircraft that crashed on our airfield boundary, the three occupants of which had departed on their sortie wearing their parade uniforms with all their decorations." This was to be the last German aircraft to crash in England, the Ju 88 G-6 coded "D5+AX," flown by a Ritterkreuzträger Hptm. Johann Dreher, Staka of 12./NJG 3. Sixteen victories were awarded to the Nachtjagd but it is probable that Dreher, not included in the lists, may have downed Lt. Terrien's aircraft before hitting trees during a ground-strafing pass at Sutton, Derwent (Yorkshire). In the end *Gisela* was not the big blow so many had hoped for. Indeed, incapable of defending German cities, *Gisela* proved to be the swansong of the Nachtjagd.

The Ju 88 G-6 flown by Oblt. Walter Briegleb, Staka of 7./NJG 2. During *Gisela*, he scored his 24th and 25th victories, the last of his career.

The crew of Oblt. Briegleb. From left: Ogfr. Rudolf Brandt, Walter Briegleb, and Ogfr. Walter Braunlich.

While three Ju 88 Gs crashed in England during *Gisela*, others were lost on their return to the continent. Maj. Berthold Ney, from the *Fernaufklärung*, and Kommandeur of IV./NJG 3, was severely injured bailing out of his Ju 88 G-6 "double chevron D5+AF" over Knesebeck, his machine having been damaged by antiaircraft fire.

## In Profile:
# Ju 88 G-6 "D5+AF" IV./NJG 3

Ju 88 G-6 Doppel Winkel "D5+AF" assigned to the *Kommandeur* IV./NJG 3 Maj. Berthold Ney. Ney was an eight-victory ace. This was a rare machine displaying fighter-style Kommandeur chevrons. It was equipped with the FuG 220 SN-2d radar with angled dipoles (frequency V). Note the FuG 350 Naxos passive homer on the roof of the canopy. Lt. Arnold Döring (10./ NJG 3) recalls:

It was as as we went to readiness during the evening of March 3, 1945 that the codeword "Gisela" finally came through. At around 23h00 a small force of some 200–300 British bombers penetrated German airspace in the region of the Münster Bight while on the ground we waited for the order to get airborne. We had on our thermal garb and had donned life jackets and stowed our life raft. Our bulky underwear and flying suits hampered our movements in the cramped cockpit of our Ju 88 G-6. Once again, we were ordered down from the aircraft—the takeoff time had been put back some 30 minutes. When we were finally ordered up—right on time—we were the third crew to launch down the runway for what had been a well-prepared and tensely awaited mission. We headed out over the North Sea, skimming the wavetops at heights of less than 50 meters to slip under the enemy's radar screen. We initially made for a radio beacon on the Dutch coast before taking up a track over the North Sea, all the while maintaining our altitude at 30–50 meters. In order to conserve fuel the throttles were set to cruise. We were looking to make landfall in the vicinity of Flamborough Head, one of the corridors leading in over England. To preserve the effect of surprise we maintained absolute radio silence. Across a wide front virtually the entire German night fighter force, aided by some bomber units, was plowing through the skies to give the British a salutary reminder that the Luftwaffe was far from beaten.

## Nachtjagd Unit Deployments, March 1945

|  |  |  |  |
|---|---|---|---|
| Stab/NJG 1 | Husum | III./NJG 5 | Blankensee |
| I./NJG 1 | Westerland | IV./NJG 5 | Greifswald |
| II./NJG 1 | Völkenrode | Stab/NJG 6 | Kitzingen |
| III./NJG 1 | Störmede | I./NJG 6 | Gross Sachsenheim |
| IV./NJG 1 | Husum | II./NJG 6 | Schwäbish-Hall |
| Stab/NJG 2 | Schleswig | III./NJG 6 | Neubiberg |
| I./NJG 2 | Eelde | IV./NJG 6 | Neubiberg |
| II./NJG 2 | Pocking | I./NJG 7 | Echterdingen/Hangelar |
| III./NJG 2 | Schleswig | II./NJG 7 | Jüterbog |
| IV./NJG 2 | Kastrup | III./NJG 7 | Leck |
| Stab/NJG 3 | Stade | 10./NJG 7 | Burg |
| I./NJG 3 | Grove | Stab/NJG 100 | Vietzkerstrand |
| II./NJG 3 | Schleswig | I./NJG 100 | Vietzkerstrand |
| III./NJG 3 | Stade | II./NJG 100 | Praque-Rusin |
| IV./NJG 3 | Nordholz | Stab/NJG 101 | Manching |
| Stab/NJG 4 | Gütersloh | I./NJG 101 | Manching |
| I./NJG 4 | Vechta | II./NJG 101 | Unterschlauerbach |
| II./NJG 4 | Gütersloh | Stab/NJG 102 | Kastrup |
| III./NJG 4 | Paderborn | I./NJG 102 | Prague-Gbell |
| Stab/NJG 5 | Blankensee | II./NJG 102 | Kastrup |
| I./NJG 5 | Altenburg | I./NJGr 10 | Liebenwalde |
| II./NJG 5 | Altenburg | | |

# To the Bitter End

In March, the NJ was awarded 176 victories, including 41 on March 7/8 and 37 on March 16/17 during two major raids on Dessau and Nuremberg. But late March/early April saw a drastic reduction in its strength, with the disbanding of the school units NJG 101 and 102. Some NJG 101 crews were transferred to Kommandeur Hptm. Martin Becker's IV./NJG 6 in Ingolstadt, but most were transferred to ground combat units. Elsewhere a further 50 combat Staffeln were dismembered. NJGs 1, 5, and 6 were reduced from eight to four Staffeln, NJGs 3, 4, and 11 from six to three; NJG 100 from four to one, while NJGr 10, Nachtst. Ungarn and Nachtst. Norwegen were also disbanded. Only NJG 2 remained complete. The Stabstaffeln were maintained. The personnel not retained, whether on the ground or in the air, were dispersed among the Flak, parachute units, or the Waffen-SS. However, several radio operators were transferred to Panzer units.

March saw the disappearance of several *Experten* and the awarding of a few decorations: on the 5th, NJG 5 Kommodore and 59-victory ace, Obstlt. Walter Borchers was killed by a Mosquito near Altenburg. On the night of March 7/8, Hptm. Hermann Greiner leading IV./NJG 1 had to abandon his aircraft over the Eifel region having run out of fuel. Wounded, he did not fly again until the end of the conflict. On the 9th, for his 48 victory claims (including numerous Mosquitos), Oblt. Kurt Welter (10./NJG 11) received the Eichenlaub. On the 13th, Hptm. Heinz Rökker (2./NJG 2—60 v.) and Hptm. Johannes Hager (6./NJG 1) received the RK for 45 successes. On the 15th, the Kommandeur of I./NJG 6, Maj. Gerhard Friedrich, a former transport pilot, was awarded the RK for 29 victories. He was killed the next day, on the night of March 16/17, near Kirchheim-Bolanden (Stuttgart) when he collided with a Lancaster.

Also on the evening of March 16/17, 1945, Lt. Erich Jung, Staka of 5./NJG 2 and his crew of radio operator Fw. Walter Heidenreich and gunner Ofw. Hans Reinnagel, were airborne at the controls of their Ju 88 G-6 "4R+AN" (WNr. 620 045) from Frankfurt-Langendiebach to intercept Bomber Command's twin-pronged assault on the southern German cities of Nuremberg and Würzberg, nearly 300 heavy bombers being assigned to strike at each. In a 30-minute period swimming in the stream Jung's crew claimed eight

On March 25, 1945, Lt. Hans Meissner (II./NJG 3) claimed his last victory, a B-24. He returned his first in January 1943 and according to one source had filed some 18 claims. Meissner is seen here in 1942 in Schleswig with his radio operator, Josef Krinner. Both bailed out safely on April 23, 1944, shot down near Bielefeld by another Nachtjäger.

On March 26/27, returning to Jever from a Nachtschlacht mission, the Ju 88 of Fw. Egon Engling (12./NJG 3) crashed on landing, having apparently touched down too early. All on board were killed. Engling was credited with seven victories. From left: Uffz. Richard März (radio operator), Fw. Egon Engling (pilot), and Uffz. Hauber (flight engineer).

Lancasters downed before returning to Zellhausen. On the 19th, Ritterkreuzträger and Eastern Front ace Engelbert Heiner, Staka of 10./NJG 6, disappeared. Leading He 219 ace Hptm Baake was also reported missing, until it was learned that he had been shot down by a Mosquito and used his ejection seat near Siegen along with his Funker Fw. Rolf Bettaque. Baake made no claims during the last four months of the war and survived. Postwar he flew for Lufthansa but was killed when he crashed Lufthansa Boeing 720 (D-ABOP) on July 15, 1964—attempting an aerobatic maneuver during a training flight, he overstressed the airframe which broke up in midair. Baake and his crew plunged to their deaths. On March 20, Hptm. Martin Becker, leading IV./NJG 6, received the Eichenlaub for 57 victories, while Hptm. Ernst-Georg Drünkler (Staka 1./NJG 5—40 v) and Lt. Karl-Ludwig Johanssen (Becker's gunner) received the RK.

Gruppenkommandeur Friedrich (white cap) at Neubiberg in July 1944 inspecting the maintenance work being carried out on the starboard BMW 801 radial of his Junkers Ju 88 G-1 coded "2Z+EH" (I./NJG 6). Note the prop blades of this engine have been turned into the *Segelstellung* or feathered position. (Paul Stipdonk)

# In Profile:
## Lt. Herbert Ludwig, Ace of 6./NJG 101

Lt. Herbert Ludwig was a leading ace in II./NJG 101, an operational training unit stationed in Unterschlauersbach west of Zirndorf. He achieved his last two kills on March 16/17, 1945 over Nuremberg during a raid in which his 6./NJG 101 Ju 88 G-6 "9W+BO" was shot down. Pilot and crew bailed out over Fischbach near Nuremberg. Ludwig was credited with 13 victories and most of his kills were achieved with BF Fw. Anton Dietrich, Uffz. Erich Gränitz (Bordmechaniker), and Ofw. Rottmann (Messfunker).

Ludwig described the events of March 16 in a letter to his wife Gertrud:

*Beim letzten Terrorangriff auf Nürnberg habe ich 2 Viermotorige in 5 Min. abgeschossen. Ich war mitten in einem Pulk, sah gleich 4 Viermotorige auf einmal* … during the last terror raid on Nuremberg I shot down two four-engine aircraft in the space of just five minutes. I was in the middle of the stream and saw four four-engine aircraft at once. I shot down two of them and was then shot down [according to Ludwig "by a Mosquito"—there were no Mosquito claims that night over Nuremberg]. My "ship" was on fire and crashed. Your sweetheart was thrown back and forth in the plane and was unable to jump clear. Then I had my upper body out of the shot-up canopy, but I was hanging helplessly in the tumbling aircraft, saw the ground rushing up to meet us and knew that the end was near. I struggled like a man possessed and suddenly I was free, hurtling through the air, calmly pulling my ripcord. The parachute came out from between my legs, there was a jolt and then I was happy. I felt so satisfied to feel blood running down my face as I floated down. In the meantime, I could hear the thumping of the flak and looking around I realized that I was right above the Reichsparteitagsgelände [stadium of the Nazi Party rallies]. I was shot down at 5,000 meters altitude and had been trapped in the burning Junkers as it fell over 3,000 meters. I don't know how I got to the ground. When I regained consciousness, I found myself being carried by soldiers on a stretcher … I only had minor scratches and bruises. Toni and Erich had already been ejected from the aircraft at 4,500 meters. Our radio operator Ofw Rottmann also got out safely but broke an ankle … There were two Mosquitoes behind me on that sortie but I shook them off, of course. However, I hadn't expected to see them over Nuremberg. Rasper shot down a four-engine aircraft the same night but was also shot down by the rear gunner. I'll be flying again in a fortnight at the latest … *Jeder Bomber, der in meinem Visier erscheint, wirft keine Bomben mehr auf Frauen und Kinder. Dieses Wort will ich halten* … every bomber that appears in my sights will drop no more bombs on women and children, I give you my word on that.

Two views of a Bf 110 discovered by the Americans at Fritzlar in May 1945 coded "9W+BO" and displaying 10 kill markings on the tailfin—nine RAF roundels and a single Soviet star. This Bf 110 was almost certainly flown by Lt. Herbert Ludwig. Two of the RAF roundels represent Halifax bombers shot down by Ludwig over Warsaw in September 1944.

# In Profile:
## Bf 110 G4, 6./NJG 101

Lt. Herbert Ludwig was an instructor and operational pilot in II./NJG 101 and flew the Bf 110, Do 217 J/N, as well as the Ju 88 G. Ludwig's 6./NJG 101 was deployed to intercept resupply missions flown for the Polish Home Army during the Warsaw Uprising. Airborne from Parndorf on the night of September 16/17, he claimed a Soviet DB–3 shot down north of Debrecen, the sole red star *Abschuss* on his scoreboard. Ludwig was officially credited with around 13 kills although in a March 1945 letter to his wife he mentioned that he was getting close to 20. On the night of March 16/17, 1945, he downed two Lancasters over Nuremberg before his Ju 88 G-6 was set alight. He and his crew bailed out with slight injuries. Note the yellow "Eastern Front" fuselage band and the 81 "meander" squiggle over the standard grays. The pattern is less tight over the wings.

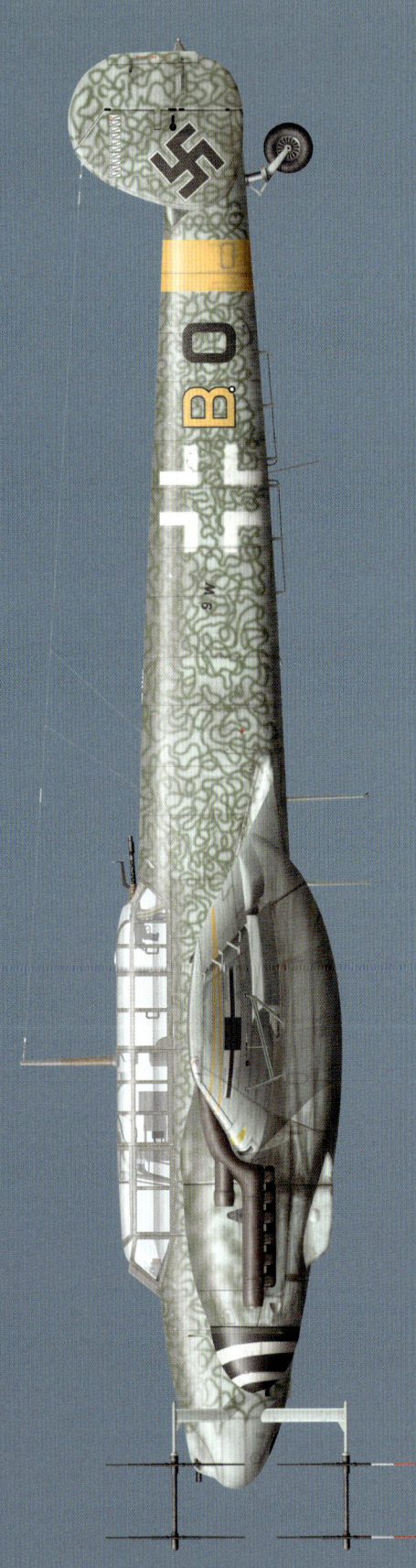

Ceremony to mark Heinz-Horst Hissbach's 100th "war flight." Having become Kommandeur of II./NJG 2, he was killed on the night of April 14/15 during a *Nachtschlachteinsatz* and was posthumously awarded the Ritterkreuz. Some older sources credit him with as many as 34 victories.

Although reduced from 88 to 37 Staffeln, the Nachtjagd continued to fight doggedly while its airfields were continually bombed or gradually captured. It is impossible to give a precise account of the *Abschüsse* during this month, as documents and confirmations are so lacking. Welter's 10./NJG 11 claimed several Mosquitos and the few pilots scored rare night victories. But often, the night fighters were engaged in *Schlachteinsätze* where many crews died.

On the night of April 14/15, Hptm. Heinz-Horst Hissbach, veteran of the *Fernnachtjagd* and Kdr of II./NJG 2, was killed with his crew near Gelnhausen during one such sortie. He was making a second pass over an American column when his aircraft took a direct hit from an antiaircraft shell and exploded. He was posthumously awarded the Ritterkreuz for his 26 victories (two by day).

On April 17, sensing that the end was nigh, the Luftwaffe High Command was quick to honor no fewer than seven NJ airmen (including two radio operators). Four Eichenlaub were awarded: Hptm. Gerhard Raht, Kommandeur of I./NJG 2, for his 58 victories; Maj. Martin Drewes, Kommandeur of III./NJG 1 and former member of ZG 76, for 49 *Luftsiege* (including four four-engine bombers by day); Maj. Herbert Lütje, Kommodore of NJG 6, for 50 victories; and Hptm. Hermann Greiner, Kommandeur of IV./NJG 1, for 51 victories.

Three Ritterkreuze were awarded: Fhj-Ofw. Anton Heinemann, radio operator for Gerhard Raht at NJG 2, for his participation in 56 *Abschüsse*; Fhj-Fw. Carlos Nugent, radio operator in Heinz Rökker's NJG 2 crew, for his participation in 62 victories; and Lt. Arnold Döring, a former KG pilot and *Wilde Sau* ace flying with NJG 3 for his 23 victories (including two B-17s).

One of the last Ritterkreuzträger of the Nachtjagd, Arnold Döring, originally from East Prussia, had a varied career. A pilot in 1940/42 with KG 53 and 55, he flew over Stalingrad and was credited with seven Soviet aircraft at the controls of his He 111. A volunteer with the *Wilde Sau*, he flew with JG 300 and then NJG 2 and 3, downing two RAF bombers over England during *Gisela*.

From April 16–25, 1945, American vehicle convoys on the A9 Berlin–Munich motorway were repeatedly targeted by *Nachtschlachter*—German night fighters flying as *Jabos* and night bombers. Aircraft from IV./NJG 6 were also involved in these attacks—including the aces from the disbanded II./NJG 101, Lt. Herbert Ludwig (13 v.), Lt. Hans Rasper (11 v.), and Oblt. Karl Dörscheln (eight kills). At around 20:30 on April 24, 1945, two Ju 88 G-6 night fighters attacked American bivouacs to the left and right of the motorway south of Lauf. A contemporary witness who observed the approach reported:

> The aircraft flew several attacks. The Americans scattered and took cover under the vehicles. After the Americans had recovered from their first scare, the aircraft, which flew another low approach, were met with wild defensive fire from hundreds of machine guns. One was hit on the third or fourth pass and pulled away at low altitude over Letten but failed to gain height and crashed into the boggy forest. The crash site is 150 meters south of today's Waldgasthof-Hotel Letten. The on-board ammunition detonated hours later during the impact fire. The crew died in the crash. One man burned to death in the aircraft, one was able to get out, but his parachute did not open fully, probably due to insufficient altitude, and he got trapped in the trees and was fatally injured. I don't remember the third man.

In the NJG 6 war diary, the April 24, 1945 entry reads, "one Ju 88 of IV./NJG 6 with crew Lt. Ludwig missing!" The pilot of the ground-strafing Ju 88 G-6 coded "9W+BO" downed near Letten was the 25-year-old Lt. Herbert Ludwig, who had also been shot down over Nuremberg on March 16, 1945.

Lt. Hans Rasper flew his last sortie of the war on April 26, 1945:

> It is now 50 years since I flew my last sortie. As a Nachtjäger I was one of the first and one of the last. I would surely already have forgotten that last sortie itself if I did not note the date—April 26—in my diary every year as the day my Bordfunker lost his life. That night 50 years ago I was shot down flying a strafing run against American columns pressing into southern Germany, managed to bail out and was taken captive. We had moved south—the enemy thought we had no fuel left—and were now based on the field at Schleißheim near Munich. The barracks had been bombed out and we lived in tents. In the evenings we were

This IV./NJG 6 Ju 88 G-6 coded "D5+NT," found abandoned by the Americans, had been converted for ground-attack sorties. To this end, the radar had been removed and bomb racks fitted. (Crow collection)

driven to the airfield and were given our mission orders. During the night our machines were topped off with fuel and around midnight we would get airborne … We could only conclude that the last throes of the war were being played out. The Americans were on the Danube and were advancing. Our nighttime missions saw us flying low-level strafing passes against American road columns. In contrast to German columns, the Americans drove with all their lights ablaze. Flying at night was already difficult enough, but at low level in the darkness of the Bavarian woods with its uneven terrain it was not at all appealing. While there was some moonlight and my eyes had got a little accustomed to the darkness, I was only at about 300 meters altitude when I was caught in a burst of enemy antiaircraft fire. As we later found out, we had been tracked for some time by radar. The starboard wing tank was immediately ablaze. I was still able to communicate with my radio operator. I told him that I was pulling up so that he could then bail out. By the time the machine stopped climbing I was getting no response from my crewman and the crate tipped over into a dive. I managed to open the escape hatch and jumped clear. At around 100 meters above the ground—I unfortunately had some jump experience—the chute opened and six or seven seconds later I came down in the treetops. I was able to slide down a tree trunk and reach firm ground. Arriving at an open field I broke into a run as I saw the burning wreck of my aircraft. An American truck got there before me—I was invited to accompany them. During my interrogation I was told that my Bordfunker's parachute had only partially deployed and that he was lying fatally injured near the aircraft. Just days later my Gruppe moved again farther south toward the Alps.

Elsewhere there were similar scenes—the huge Soviet columns on the eastern approaches to Berlin did not douse their headlights either, as NJG 100 ace Oblt. Günther Bertram recorded:

Born in Mannheim on October 8, 1911, Hans Rasper was one of the first aces of the Nachtjagd—between December 1940 and January 1942 he was credited with seven confirmed kills in NJG 1. Early in 1943 he was transferred to II./NJG 101 as an instructor. He claimed an eighth victory on the night of March 16/17, 1945, over Nuremberg.

This Ju88 G-6 coded "D5+DP" had its AI aerials removed and was flown by Hptm. Werner Büchter, St.Kpt. of 6./NJG 3, as a *Nachtschlachter*. (via Theo Boiten)

> We were based on fields in Pomerania as we fell back and because of a shortage of fuel the relatively few sorties that were flown were primarily night ground-attack missions against the never-ending Russian supply columns that wound their way, headlights ablaze, to the front. We approached the front at altitude, shut down our engines and glided silently toward the columns of trucks and vehicles. Each night that skies were clear and the moon bright, our 2-cm cannon wrought death and destruction against these targets. This was one way we night fighters could bring some relief to our hard-pressed ground troops. But even sorties like this had little impact on the Russian advance as they pressed on toward Berlin. Meanwhile RAF and USAAF bombers dropped their cargoes unhindered. Neither the German day- nor night-fighter force could put up any serious opposition. Day bomber formations had powerful escorts and even at night long-range Mosquito intruders screened the bombers. We could not even operate from our remaining operational aerodromes without Mosquito intruders appearing over the field, rendering takeoffs impossible. On one occasion I did manage to get airborne and was able to close on a bomber formation returning homeward over Bitterfeld. I was able to down a Lancaster at 5,000 meters altitude for my 35th and last victory (on the evening of April 10, 1945). From Wittstock an der Dosse we moved northward to Lübeck where we blew up our aircraft and where the crews were taken into captivity. On release I made my way to Hamburg which was not too distant. My wife and my parents welcomed me home, glad that I—a husband and son—was safe and well and had survived uninjured.

On April 28, the last two Ritterkreuze were awarded to two Nachtjagd aces: Hptm. Fritz Lau, initially a transport pilot and then a blind-flying instructor, led 9. and then 4./NJG 1 in 1943, with 28 victories to his credit (27 four-engine aircraft and 1 Mosquito), and Austrian Maj. Hubert Rauh, Kdr of II./NJG 4, was belatedly rewarded for his 31 victories—including no less than 29 *Viermots*.

According to T. Boiten's research, the Nachtjagd's last victory was on May 2/3, 1945, when Oblt. Fritz Brandt of the Stab/NJG 3 shot down a Halifax from 199 Sqn north of Hamburg, his eighth *Abschuss*.

Inexorably, the remaining night fighter units were captured by the Western Allies and the Soviets. Some crews were able to escape, such as the III./NJG 5 Ju 88 (coded "C9+AR") piloted by Hptm. Werner Hopf, Staka of 8./NJG 5 (21 victories). Hopf landed in Dübendorf on the morning of April 30 with three officers, two women and a 6-year-old child on board. Or WNr 621800 of 7./NJG 2, which reached Pedras Rubras in Portugal on May 2, 1945.

According to Martin Drewes, his III./NJG 1 waited in Husum for the arrival of the Allied forces. A week after the German surrender, Canadian and then British troops appeared and evacuated the airfield. They were hardly interested in the Bf 110s, probably preferring to study the Me 163s on the runway. At most, the propellers were ordered to be removed to prevent takeoffs. One of Drewes's radio operators from the Sudetenland had not waited for this happen—with a pilot who was also from Czechoslovakia, he had flown to Sweden after "stealing" a Bf 110. After three or four weeks of semi-liberty, Drewes and his comrades were released to start a new life. Fw. Hasso von Zieten of II./NJG 101 remembers the times:

> we remained in Unterschlauersbach until the end and only departed the airfield when the fuel had run out and our "crates" were being blown up. Those crews still on the airfield had brand-new Ju 88 G-6 night fighters which were flown to Ingolstadt-Manching. Just an hour after arriving here we witnessed the most spectacular fireworks display. There was nothing for us in Manching. We had no aircraft. We hitchhiked our way to Munich. After two cars were shot out from under us, we arrived in Neubiberg. They wanted to put us in the infantry there, but at the last minute there was a chance for further flying action. Bertsche (also Fw. and *Kutscher* in 5. Staffel) was still with me. They were looking for volunteers for what they called a risky mission in the south or east. Well, that was my "*Heimat*," so we both volunteered. We were isolated and kept under guard in a building on the airfield and sworn in again. Then the purpose was announced: with those "mills" still available around Munich, from Ju 88 night fighters to the Bü 181, *Unternehmen Bienenstock* was to be launched from the jumping-off fields of Graz or Klagenfurt. [Operation *Beehive* was a plan for sabotage and supply interdiction sorties to be flown behind Allied lines.] One night we boarded a bus and were driven to Fürstenfeldbruck—but when we got there, everybody had already evacuated and there was no fuel. Just hours later American tanks would be on the airfield. In the woods around the field, we discovered many aircraft—some without props. One Bü 181 had a tank of petrol, even the seat chute was untouched. It was not until we were in the air that it occurred to me that I could be put up against a wall and shot for this—no map, no flight plan, no orders. We put down in Prien am Chiemsee where my story about *Bienenstock* was believed—they had heard about the "Sonderkommando." We were given authorization to fly onto Klagenfurt. We

Hasso von Zieten of II./NJG 101 (left) with his crew, BF Hubert Ungerbock and BM Hohensee in front of their Me 110 G night fighter during conversion training in Parndorf, October 1944.

made an intermediate stop in Aigen im Ennstal to call in on my mother, before carrying on to Klagenfurt. We didn't quite make it. We ran out of fuel and had to make an emergency landing. We finally arrived in Klagenfurt by road … at the same time as the British. The date was May 8, 1945. *Für mich war der Krieg zu Ende*.

Three views of Herbert Koch's Ju 88 G-6 coded "D5+AH" seen at Grove during the last month of the war. Koch had been appointed Staffelkapitän of 1./NJG 3 in August 1944. Note the ventral *Waffenbehälter* (weapons tray) toting MG 151/20 cannon and the inscription "*Komm Zuruck*" on the open lower fuselage access hatch, the title of a popular song of the period, a plea to come home safely. The individual letter "A" has been neatly outlined and is repeated on the nose. (via Paul Stipdonk)

## In Profile:
# Ju 88 G-6 "D5+AH", 1./NJG 3

Junkers Ju 88 G-6 coded "D5+AH" (WNr. 621796) flown by Hptm. Herbert Koch, Staffelkapitän of 1./NJG 3. Operating out of Grove, Denmark during April 1945, Koch and his crew downed an RAF Coastal Command Halifax on the night of April 24/25, 1945 over the North Sea for their 23rd and last *Luftsieg*—one of the last *Nachtjagd Viermot* victories of the war. Note the 20 *Abschussbalken* on the tailfin scoreboard, the yellow lower engine cowl covers and mottled spinners. The air intercept radar was the FuG 220 Lichtenstein SN-2d with obliquely mounted dipoles and associated tail-warning radar mounted under the rudder.

Terminal Decline: January–May 1945

Wearing his RK, Ofw. Eduard Lindinger (right) is photographed after crash-landing his 9./NJG 5 Ju 88 G-6 coded "C9+ET" following an undercarriage malfunction at Lüneberg or Lübeck in the last months of the war. Lindinger had won the Ritterkreuz for over 300 sorties in KG 1 but returned no night victories while in III./NJG 5. He survived the war and died on September 1, 2004. (via Michael Meyer)

# Afterword

The Nachtjagd has fascinated many readers—with some reason. The particular "defensive" character of this branch of the Luftwaffe and its remarkable personalities, especially its aces (Lent, Falck, Schnaufer et al.), its increasingly sophisticated aircraft (Bf 110 G-4, Ju 88 G-6), its innovative detection equipment (SN-2), its constantly revised tactics—all these aspects have been studied and scrutinized. Few, however, have highlighted its great weakness: its "adolescence." Unlike the other military air forces of World War II, the Luftwaffe was continually short of personnel and reservists, since it only came into being in 1934. The same applied to the embryonic night fighter arm, which did not exist prior to 1940. While many of its airmen proved to be extremely competent, from mid-1941 (see *Night Fighter Aces of the Luftwaffe 1940–43*, page 50) there were major difficulties in raising new units or even training young crews to fly on instruments. The Nachtjagd recruited *Zerstörer*, bomber, transport and reconnaissance pilots, but this was not enough, and the problem got worse. The Kammhuber Line, a defensive curtain designed to protect the Ruhr, Berlin, and cities in northern Germany, could not be extended into France due to a lack of personnel and resources. As with the Tagjagd, the night fighter arm distinguished itself by achieving major successes in the early years of the war but, from 1943 onward, it began an inexorable decline when it was confronted with the enemy's numerical superiority. This was followed by exaggerated overclaims (as early as August 1943) and the "anarchic" deployment of units sent hither and thither, often without logic.

This continual lack of manpower prevented the Nachtjagd from inflicting losses of around 10 percent, a rate that would have been sufficient to stem the RAF's night-bombing offensive. The crews' task was further complicated in June 1944 when, after D-Day, the Nachtjagd, essentially a defensive weapon, had to go on the offensive, being engaged throughout the last year of its existence in deadly and costly *Nachtschlachteinsätze*. Despite all this, right up to the end, even with a cruel lack of fuel, aircraft and personnel, the Nachtjäger fought the crews of Bomber Command with the energy of despair.

# References and Further Reading

Aders, Gebhard. *German Night Fighter Force 1917–1945* (Fonthill Media, 2016).
Bates, H. E. *Night Fighter: The Battle Against Hitler's Night Raiders 1940–1941* (Air World, 2024).
Becker, Hans-Jürgen. *Schwere Jäger und Zerstörer der Luftwaffe* (Motorbuch, 1999).
Boiten, Theo. *The Nachtjagd War Diaries* (2 vols, Red Kite, 2008), personal accounts translated by Neil Page.
Bundesarchiv RL/10 files, various.
Bundrock, Kurt. *Kampf am nächtlichen Himmel, Einsatzerlebnisse eines Ritterkreuzträgers der Nachtjagd* (Der Landser).
Engau, Fritz. *Frontal durch die Bomberpulks* (Grax, Hoppe, 1997).
Falck, Wolfgang. *Falkenjahre—Erinnerungen 1910–2003* (296 Verlag, 2003).
Ferguson, R. *Heinkel He 219: An illustrated history of the Third Reich's dedicated home defense night fighter* (Red Kite, 2022).
*Jägerblatt* (journal of the German fighter pilots association), various issues, including the "Fernnachtjäger" series by Mölenbeck and the II./NJG 1 war diary by Diener.
Lorant, Jean-Yves. *Jagdgeschwader 300* (2 vols, Eagle Editions, 2005), translated by Neil Page.
Martínez, Eduardo Manuel Gil. *Guide to German Night Fighters in World War II: The Night Defenders of the Reich* (Connoisseur's Books, 2022).
Matthews, J. & Foreman, J. *Luftwaffe Aces* (4 vols, Red Kite 2014).
Mölenbeck, Otto. *Ferne Nachtjagd* (Motorbuch, 1978).
Obermaier, Ernst. *Die Ritterkreuzträger der Luftwaffe 1939–1945* (Dieter Hoffmann, 1966).
Page, Neil & Roba, Jean-Louis. *Night Fighter Aces of the Luftwaffe, 1940–43* (Casemate, 2025).
Page, Neil. *Luftwaffe Fighters: Combat on All Fronts* (2 vols, Mortons, 2021).
Ries, Karl & Obermaier, Ernst. *Bilanz am Seitenleitwerk* (Dieter Hoffmann 1970).
Roba, Jean-Louis. *The Luftwaffe in Africa* (Casemate, 2019).
Roba, Jean-Louis. *La Luftwaffe en Belgique* (2 vols, Lela Presse, 2021).
Roba, Jean-Louis. *La Luftwaffe en France 1939–45* (2 vols, Éditions Arès, 2022).
Roba, Jean-Louis. *La Chasse de Nuit allemande en Roumanie* (Bucharest, 1994).
Saintes, Philippe. *Luftwaffe Victory Markings 1939–45* (Casemate, 2022).
Spoden, Peter. *Ich war Nachtjäger in Göring's Luftwaffe* (self-published, 2007).
Stipdonk, P. & Meyer, M. *Die Deutsche Luftwaffe—Zerstörer- und Nachtjägerverbände* (4 vols, VDM Heinz Nickel).
Williams, David. *Nachtjäger Luftwaffe Night Fighter Units 1939–45* (Classic Publications, 2021).
Zorner, Paul. *Nächte im Bomberstrom: Erinnerungen 1920–1950* (NeunundzwanzigSechs-Verlag, 2007).

# Index

346 (French) Sqn), 97

Altenburg, 28, 112–13
Altendorf, Rudolf, 22–23
Altner, Herbert, 100
Arndt, Wilfried, 22
Athies, 23, 57, 64–65, 69
Augenstein, Hans-Heinz, 53, 70, 97
Autenrieth, Hans, 48, 68

Baake, Werner, 8, 50, 74–75, 78, 106, 114
Baer, Hans, 18
Bahr, Günther, 30, 51, 107
Baranovichi, 8, 88
Bauer, Martin, 13, 83, 86
Becker, Martin "Tino," 7, 62, 113–14
Bellinghausen, Theodor, 81
Bergen, Uffz. von, 32
Berger, Friedrich, 37
Bergmann, Helmut, 61–63, 66, 68
Berlin, 7–8, 10, 24–25, 31–32, 34–60
Bertram, Günther, 11, 89, 119
*Blindschleiche* sorties, 38
Blumensaat, Albert, 43
Bochum, Allied raids on, 27, 36, 95, 97
Bonin, Eckart-Wilhelm von, 32, 36, 51, 53
Borchers, Walter, 47, 67, 96, 113
*Bordsuchgeräte* onboard search radar, 32
Braham, Bob, 24, 28
Brandis, 23, 26, 35, 44, 57, 60, 64
Brandy, Fritz, 9, 120
Brandt, Rudolf, 52, 110
Bräunlich, Walter, 52, 110
Braunschweig (Brunswick), USAAF raid on, 48, 63
Bremen, Allied raids on, 29, 37, 75, 95
Bremerhaven, RAF raid on, 93
Briegleb, Walter, 52, 66, 71, 110
Bryansk, 13, 44
Bucharest-Otopeni, 84, 86
Bundrock, Kurt, 71
Bunje, Helmut, 59

Caen, 69
Cambrai, 66, 70
Cannes, RAF raid on, 30
Chemnitz and Rositz, RAF raid on, 107
Cologne, RAF raid on, 32
Coulommiers, 64–66, 68–70

Dahms, Helmut, 89
Darmstadt, RAF raid on, 76, 93
D-Day see Normandy Campaign
de Miremont, Alexander "Axel" Graf Rességuier, 15, 106
Deelen, 33, 44, 60, 63–65, 73, 91
Derlitzki, Uffz., 33
Dessau, Allied raid on, 113
Dittmann, Gerhard, 24

Doelfs, Walter, 24–25
Döring, Arnold, 95, 108, 111, 117
Dörscheln, Karl, 118
Dortmund, RAF raids on, 63, 95, 97
Dortmund–Ems Canal, 93, 97
Dresden, RAF raid on, 9, 107
Drewes, Martin, 28, 47, 71, 73–74, 117, 121
Drünkler, Ernst-Georg, 68, 114
Dübendorf, Swiss impound Bf 110 G-4 "2Z+OP" at, 55–56, 120–21
Düding, Fw., 88
Dunkirk, 46, 54
Düsseldorf, RAF raid on, 30, 32, 62, 91, 95–97

Ebhardt, Rolf, 38–39, 62
Echterdingen, 8, 27, 43–44, 55, 64–65, 73, 84, 91, 112
Ehle, Walter, 7, 25–26, 30–33
Engel, Walter, 108
Engling, Egon, 114
Ernst, Lt., 32–33
Essen, Allied raid on, 60, 62

Fellerer, Leopold, 61
Fengler, Georg, 61, 95–96
*Fernnachtjagd* sorties, 52, 69, 95, 106, 117
Finkeldey, Martin, 98
Finster, Oblt., 32
Fischer, August, 88
Florennes, 19, 21–23, 26, 34, 41, 44–46, 53–54, 57, 63–65, 71, 77, 93
Focsani, 15, 65, 84–85
Forke, Hannes, 34–35, 45, 52–55
Frank, Heinz-Dieter, 28, 77
Frank, Rudolf, 52, 61–62, 96
Frankfurt am Main, Allied raids on, 29, 33–35, 38, 50, 56, 93
Fransci, Gustav, 8, 87–89
French Resistance, 55, 63–64
Freymann, Oblt., 31
Friedrich, Gerhard, 113–14
Friedrichshafen, Allied raid on, 62
FuG 220 Lichtenstein radar system, 32, 40, 56, 58, 72, 80, 111, 123
FuG 227 Flensburg radar homer, 58, 72

Gajewski, Johannes, 37
Gänsler, Wilhelm, 74, 96
Geiger, August, 28
Göring, Hermann, 9, 20, 25, 27, 94, 99
Granderath, Jakob, 102
Greiner, Hermann, 51–52, 55, 67, 74, 93, 97, 113, 117
Grimm, Heinz, 24, 29
Grove, 44, 51, 103, 112, 122–23
Gunselmann, Karl, 15
Györy, August, 105

# Index

Habicht, Fritz, 79, 106
Hagen, RAF raid on, 28
Hagenau, 62, 64–65
Hager, Johannes, 32, 113
Halberstadt, USAAF raid on, 47–48
Hamburg, Allied raid on *see also* Operation *Gomorrah*, 6, 10, 18, 97, 104, 120
Hangelar, 32, 44, 51, 92, 96, 112
Hanover, Allied raids on, 27, 29, 32, 50–52, 106
Harris, Arthur "Bomber," 7, 34
Heidenreich, Walter, 68, 113
Heilbronn, RAF raid on, 98
Heinemann, Anton, 117
Heiner, Engelbert, 16, 99, 114
Heise, Uffz., 31
Helbig flyers (LG 1), 27
Hemskerck, Henrik von, 14
Henning, Horst, 94–95
Henseler, Lt., 32
Herget, Wilhelm, 36, 38, 62, 66, 70–71, 74
Herrmann, Hans-Joachim "Hajo," 7, 20, 25, 77
  JG Herrman, 15, 18, 24–25, 106
*Himmelbett* system, 31
Hissbach, Heinz-Horst, 117
Hitler, Adolf, 88
Hoffman, Werner, 47, 67
Hoffmann, Uffz., 33
Hohensee, BM, 121
Holler, Otto, 81
Hörwick, Anton "Balbo," 107
Huchler, Otto, 68
Husemann, Werner, 94, 96, 98

Jabs, Hans-Joachim, 18, 55, 61, 63, 71, 75, 93
*Jägerblatt*, 78
Jever, 101, 114
Johanssen, Karl-Ludwig, 7, 114
Johnen, Wilhelm, 52, 62, 84, 96–97
Jung, Erich, 9, 40, 68, 113
Junkers, 58, 77–78
Jurleit, Manfred, 99
Jüterbog, 44, 91, 98–99, 112

Kammhuber Line, 124
Kammhuber, Josef, 10, 26, 31, 77–78
Kark, Werner, 42, 95
Karlsruhe, RAF raid on, 41, 62, 98
Kassel, RAF raids on, 28–29
Kassel-Rothwesten, 40, 44, 57, 69
Kern, Karl, 64–65
Kiel, Allied raids on, 37, 47, 50, 73, 75–76, 93
Kitzingen, 43–44, 64–65, 71, 91, 103, 112
Koch, Herbert, 122–23
Koch, Robert, 95
Kock, Uffz., 32
Kociok, Josef, 13–14, 17
Kollak, Reinhard, 66
Kollak, Walter, 25–26, 31, 53
Königsberg, RAF raid on, 76–77, 89, 92, 107
Konter, Helmut, 87
Kotschote, Günther, 105

Kraft, Georg, 24, 51, 93–94
Krahforst, Josef, 61, 64
Krause, Hans, 106–7
Kubisch, Walter, 42–43, 95
Kursk, battle of, 11, 13
Kurzwernhart, Gottfried, 41

Le Culot, 70, 75
Lechner, Alois, 15, 82
Leipzig, RAF raid on, 29, 36, 52
Lent, Helmut, 9, 19–20, 36, 42–43, 53, 66–68, 75, 94–95, 124
Leuchs, Rolf, 27
Leverkusen, RAF raid on, 8, 34, 78
Lhose, Heinz, 53
Liebherr, Hans, 74
Linke, Oblt., 32
Lippe-Weißenfeld, Egmont Prinz zur, 19–20, 37
Lommatzsch, Reinhard, 100
Lübeck, 120, 124
Ludwig, Herbert, 115–16, 118
Ludwigshafen, 7, 26, 30, 34, 41, 47
Luedecke, Ofw., 32
Lufthansa, 75, 82, 88, 114
Luftministerium, 63
Lüneburg, 29, 47
Lütje, Herbert, 87, 83–85, 117

Mäckle, Hans, 58, 72
Magdeburg, 48, 100
Mainz-Finthen, 21, 44, 64–65, 91
Mannheim, RAF raids on, 21, 26–27, 33
März, Richard, 114
Meien, Ulrich von, 85
Meister, Ludwig, 23, 34–35, 45–46, 52–57, 70
Metz, 44, 53, 55, 57
Meurer, Manfred, 19–20, 30, 36, 48, 77
Milan, RAF raid on, 19
Milch, Erhard, 77
Mitteland Canal, 97, 107
Modrow, Ernst-Wilhelm, 62, 66, 71, 75, 80, 106
Morlock, Wilhelm "Willi," 97
Müller, Friedrich-Karl "Nasen," 24–25, 74, 90, 92
Müller, Hans-Hermann, 53
Münchengladbach, 25, 93

Nabrich, Josef, 78, 79, 106
Nachtjagdversuchskommando (NJVK, Night Fighter Test Detachment), 77
*Nachtschlachteinsätze* sorties, 9, 68–69, 101, 124
Ney, Berthold, 110–11
Niebelschütz, Hans-Wolfgang von, 19
Noirot, Marcel, 109
Normandy Campaign, 8, 60–80, 124
Nowarra, Heinz, 78
Nuremberg, RAF raids on, 8–9, 21, 25, 31, 60–61, 96, 113, 115–16, 118

Oberhausen, RAF raid on, 96
Operation *Bagration*, 8, 88
Operation *Bodenplatte*, 6, 9, 105, 108

127

Operation *Gisela*, 6, 9, 108–11, 117
Operation *Gomorrah*, 6, 18, 21, 35–36
Operation *Heidelberg*, 68
Operation *Tidal Wave*, 6, 15, 84
Operation *Wacht am Rhein*, 6, 9, 101
Operation *Zitadelle*, 13
Orscha, 14, 44, 87
Oschersleben, USSAF raid on, 47–48
Ostheimer, Fw., 49

Pas-de-Calais, 63, 66–67
*Pauke, Pauke—Nachrichtenblatt eines Jagdkorps*, 37
Peenemünde, 24–25
Peters, Erhard, 25, 52
Pietrek, Norbert, 22
Ploesti oilfields, 6, 8, 15, 84
Polish Resistance, 8, 88
Pützkuhl, Josef, 87–89

Radusch, Günther, 18, 25, 36, 51, 61, 67
RAF Bomber Command, 7–9, 19, 21, 25, 27, 29–30, 34–36, 40, 47, 52, 60, 63, 66–69, 71, 73, 75–77, 92–94, 96–98, 100, 107, 109, 113, 124
    205 Group, 8, 84, 88
    Light Night Striking Force (LNSF), 8, 10, 78, 99
Raht, Gerhard, 37, 52, 71, 117
Rasper, Hans, 115, 118–19
Rauh, Hubert, 41, 120
Red Army, 88, 106–7
Rheydt, RAF raid on, 25, 93
Rhine River, 97
Richter, Johannes, 94
Riedelberger, Walter, 101
Rökker, Heinz, 67, 69, 74, 96–97, 113, 117
Romanian Air Force (FARR), 15, 85
Rumpelhardt, Fritz, 32, 37–38, 96
Rüsselsheim, RAF raid on, 75–76

Sayn-Wittgenstein, Heinrich zu, 8, 12–13, 35, 45, 48–49
Scheer, Klaus, 8, 81, 89
Scheibe, Gerhard, 36, 48
Scherfling, Karl-Heinz, 24, 61, 72–73
Schierholz, Hans-Georg, 96, 98
Schlacht arm, 6, 18
Schleswig, 42, 44, 60, 91, 95, 104, 112–13
Schnaufer, Heinz-Wolfgang, 32, 37–38, 43, 51–52, 61–62, 66, 71, 74–75, 93, 95–96, 108, 124
Schneeweiss, Wolfgang, 11
Schneidewind, Wilhelm, 21
Schoenert, Rudolf, 14, 18, 51, 62, 82, 93–94
*Schräge Musik* cannon, 11–12, 37, 47, 53, 58, 87
Schweinfurt and Regensburg, RAF raids on, 6, 21
Semrau, Paul, 67, 96, 107
Sigmund, Rudolf, 19, 28
Sint-Denijs-Westrem, 22
Smolensk, 11, 14, 44
Soika, Alfred, 97
Sommer, Hermann, 51–52
Söthe, Fritz, 66–67, 93
Spanish Civil War, 16, 107
St.-Dizier, 28, 44, 51, 55, 57, 64–65, 69

St.-Trond (Sint-Truiden), 7, 26, 30–33, 44, 57, 63–65, 75, 91, 95
Stade, 42, 44, 65, 70, 76, 91, 104, 112
Steinamanger, 64, 84, 91
Sterkrade factory, Allied raid on, 71, 75
Stettin, RAF raid on, 47, 75, 77
Streib, Werner, 33, 55, 71
Strohecker, Karl, 81, 87
Strüning, Heinz, 26, 71, 77, 101
Stuttgart, and RAF raids on, 8, 26, 29, 34, 35–36, 53, 55, 73, 93, 96
Stuttgart-Echterdingen, 44
*Sumatra I* radar train, 82, 87
*Sumatra III* radar train, 87
Swiss Air Force, 55–56, 62
Szameitat, Paul, 36, 46

Tallinn, and Soviet raid on, 81
Targsorul Nou, 84–85
Telge, Wilhelm, 26, 31
Thun, Rudolf, 55
Thurow, Günther, 106–7
Turin, RAF raid on, 19

Uhlmann, Werner, 19, 21
Ungerbock, Hubert, 121
U.S. Army, 97
USAAF, 6, 8, 15, 21, 30, 37–38, 50, 84–85, 88, 120
    Eighth Air Force, 22, 29
    Fifteenth Air Force, 84

V1 launch sites, 8, 66–67, 71
Vechta, 44, 57, 60, 65, 70, 101, 112
Vegesack, USAAF raid on, 29
Venlo, 44, 54, 62, 65, 79–80, 84, 91, 106
*Verfolgungsnachtjagd* sorties, 58
Vinke, Heinz, 24–25, 27, 50, 52, 54
Vornhusen, Uffz., 32
Vries, Heinz de, 88

Wagner, Gerhard, 68
Waldenberger, Walter, 15
Waldhelm, Jürgen, 18
Warsaw Uprising, 8, 88–89, 116
Weißflog, Erich, 71
Welter, Kurt (Kommando Welter), 9, 27, 50, 93, 96, 99–100, 113, 117
Wesseling and Scholven, RAF raids on, 71
*Wilde Sau*, 7, 15, 20, 25–28, 30–31, 44, 50, 52, 77, 90, 99, 108, 117
Wilhelmshaven, RAF raid on, 96
Wilke, Heinrich, 47, 97
Window (chaff, *Düppel*), 26, 31, 35, 68
Winkler, Herbert, 72
Wittmer, Heiner, 99
Woeste, Achim, 76
Wohlers, Heinrich, 8, 43, 55
Würzburg radar system, 11, 15, 88

*Zahme Sau*, 10, 26, 49, 58
Zieten, Hasso von, 121
Zöller, Uffz., 31
Zorner, Paul, 36, 47, 52–53, 66–67, 70, 93, 97